HOW to be
an *ALIEN*
in *ENGLAND*

HOW to be an *ALIEN* in *ENGLAND*

A Guide to the English

Angela Kiss

1 3 5 7 9 10 8 6 4 2

First published in 2016 by September Publishing

Copyright © Angela Kiss 2016

The right of Angela Kiss to be identified as the author of this work has been asserted by her in accordance with the Copyright Designs and Patents Act 1988.

Illustration copyright © Stephanie von Reiswitz 2016

Quotes in the text from George Mikes' books *How to be a Brit* (Penguin Books, 1986) and *English Humour for Beginners* (Penguin Books, 1983), reproduced by permission of Penguin Books Ltd.

Typeset by Ed Pickford

Printed in Poland on paper from responsibly managed, sustainable sources by Hussar Books

ISBN 978-1-910463-21-5

September Publishing
www.septemberpublishing.org

HOW to be
an *ALIEN*
in *ENGLAND*

CONTENTS

1 How to be an alien   1

2 How to be optimistic   5

3 How to love 11

4 How to live with others. 19

5 How to fake it if you cannot make it. 27

6 How to Keep Calm and Carry On 33

7 How to talk about the weather 39

8 How to imagine queuing. 45

9 How to mind your own business. 49

10 How not to use a hot-water bottle. 55

11 How not to lose your superpower 63

12 How to blame. 71

13 How to kiss in the rain 77

14 How English humour doesn't exist 83

15 How to work. 89

16 How to be polite 95

17 How to interpret the English language 103

18 How to make The English feel uneasy 111

19 How to commute 119

21 How to dine 127

22 How to understand understatement and
    underachievement 129

23 How to have a holiday 135

24 How to be equal 143

25 How to fake modern English 147

26 How to be a dinner guest in England 157

27 How to date 167

28 How to write a love letter to England 175

29 How to be arrogant 181

Afterword 191

1

HOW TO BE AN ALIEN

Before I moved to London I never thought of myself as an alien. But, since then, being an alien has become my number one personality trait.

To help me cope with myself as an alien, my brother Attila presented me with a book, George Mikes' *How to be an Alien*. It was published in 1946, when the term 'alien' was commonly used to describe foreigners. When I look at the mirror it still seems just right.

The book was translated into 22 languages, sold in 39 countries and has now sold over 450,000 copies. It is not an exaggeration to say that it was (and still is) a worldwide bestseller. Of course the best compliment George Mikes could get from The English was that his book was 'not too bad'.

That George was accepted, and became a bestselling writer, gave me hope. And reading the first few pages I had the feeling that if George was still alive we would definitely be friends. Not best friends, since everyone knows that in London your best friend is your umbrella, but second-best friends. Because we have so much in common.

First of all, we are both Hungarians. George was born a mere 70 kilometres away from where I was born. (No, sorry, I have no idea how many miles that is.) We both fled from Hungary. (Okay, he fled due to political reasons while I fled from a broken heart, but still.) George planned to stay only temporarily and then move on, but he lived in England for the rest of his life, and my short stay too has already extended for a decade.

For me, this and Mikes' other books seemed the perfect way to help me understand both myself as an alien and also The English. And it did help a lot.

However, some things have changed since 1946, and although George and I have many similarities in our lives, we have many differences too. First of all he was a man and I am a woman, and everybody

Of course the best compliment George Mikes
could get from The English was that his book
was 'not too bad'.

knows that men and women see the same things quite differently, sometimes completely oppositely. Also, when George arrived to England he was already quite proficient in English while I couldn't speak a word, therefore he had a good job making documentaries for the BBC, while my first job was serving tables in a kebab shop 72 hours a week for £600 per month. So I thought that, just like he did, I shall challenge myself to examine The English and learn how not to be a too bad alien.

Why?

Because George was completely right, saying: 'The world still consists of two clearly divided groups: the English and the foreigners. One group consists of less than 50 million people; the other of 3,950 million. The latter group does not really count.'

2

HOW TO BE OPTIMISTIC

I WAS EXTREMELY ENTHUSIASTIC to learn optimism from The English when I moved to London.

You may ask why?

Well, because I am Hungarian.

We are said to be the most pessimistic people in Europe. Probably in the whole planet. Moon included. Hungarians always see the worst. If something is good it is suspicious for us. The common belief in Hungary is that an optimistic person is simply uninformed. Or misinformed.

Of course we agree that optimism would be a better approach to life but it is just not our thing. It has never been.

For example, have you ever heard the Hungarian national anthem? No? Good for you! I wouldn't recommend it at all. Unless you are looking for inspiration for your suicide attempt. If it is not just an attempt but you are deadly serious about your suicide then I strongly recommend you not only read the lyrics but listen to the music too. The most mournful funeral song sounds jolly compared to it.

Other nations have inspiring anthems like 'God Save the Queen' or 'La Marseillaise' or 'The Star-Spangled Banner', and their lyrics are about victory and proudness like 'Russia – our sacred home-land, Russia – our beloved country' or 'Germany, Germany above everything, Above everything in the world!'

But what about the Hungarian anthem?

It starts with 'O Lord, bless the Hungarian' and then follow eight long and painful stanzas about our 'slave yoke' and 'funeral urn' and 'the corpses of our defeated army' and 'groans of death, weeping' and finally it finishes with 'Pity, O Lord, the Hungarians they who have suffered for all sins of the past and of the future!'

Yes, of the future too.

It doesn't sound optimistic, does it?

Plus to multiply our pessimism we have a tradition that on New Year's Eve at midnight every single Hungarian in the whole world stands up and sings our happy-go-lucky national anthem.

Perfect start for a new year, isn't it?

There are those lunatic people who always prophesy the end of the world. I belong to them. I strongly believe that the end of the world will come as a worldwide mass suicide when one day Hungary wins all the Olympic gold medals and the whole world is constantly forced to listen to our national anthem. Don't laugh! There is a fair chance of that since we are amongst the top countries of the Olympic medal table. If you consider the population of the other countries, actually we are second after Finland. So, as you can see, I am not kidding.

Now I am sure you understand why I wanted to learn optimism from The English. They seemed like the perfect nation to teach me how to 'always look on the bright side of life'.

I needed optimism. A lot.

But soon I realised that The English are not entirely optimistic. But I wouldn't say that they are pessimistic either.

So what are they?

To be honest even a decade in England is not enough for me to find the right word to describe their temperament, so I have had no other option but to invent a new expression myself, to contribute to the English language.

In my opinion The English are 'borderline pessimistic'.

For evidence of my borderline pessimist theory there is only one word you have to understand. This word is the English favourite national catchphrase, namely: 'typical'.

Let's say it rains all bank holiday weekend. Are The English surprised or sad or angry?

Not at all. Because this is what they have expected and this is what happened.

They only sigh philosophically, with a look of a prophet who is prideful that his (in this case: negative) prognostication has happened, and they say: 'Typical.' (With a dot and not with an exclamation mark.)

In England everything is typical. If your train is late, it is typical. If there are no seats on the upper deck of a bus, it is typical. If the printer breaks down at your workplace just before you want to use it, it is typical. If it starts to rain at five o'clock just before you leave work, it is typical. If you pay £4 for a £3 meal deal, it is typical. If there are severe delays on the tube because of suicide, it is typical. If your meal is late, cold or uneatable in a restaurant, it is typical. If your queue is the slowest queue, it is typical. If you wake up at the weekend because of the noise of your neighbour's lawn-mower, it is typical. For The English everything is typical. And not just small everyday things but big things too. One of my English friends said that the American Revolution was so typical of the bloody Americans. (Sorry, Americans, but you must know the truth: The English call you 'bloody' too; in their eyes you are no better than any other alien nation.) When I asked my friend how it could be typical if it was the first and last and *only* War of American Independence, he looked at me as puzzled as if I was an alien from a faraway unknown planet. (Or at least from Hungary.) And after his long, puzzled pause he did not answer, of course. Which was so typical of The English! (Typical *with* exclamation mark!)

For me the constant use of the word 'typical' sounds more pessimistic than optimistic. It is like always seeing the worst. With not as much pessimism as Hungarians, but definitely borderline pessimistic.

But there is nothing wrong with pessimism. The world needs pessimism too. There is a well-known aphorism by G.B. Stern: 'Both optimists and pessimists contribute to our society. The optimist invents the airplane and the pessimist the parachute.'

Have you ever heard the story of Robert Cocking?

He was an English parachute designer and developer. (For your information: the modern parachute was invented by a Frenchman. I am just adding it to please French readers and give them a chance to look down upon The English more than they already do.)

Despite being a parachute developer, the English Robert Cocking was not a pessimist at all. He was an optimist. He was certain that his new parachute design would work. So believed the large audience in Vauxhall Gardens.

But sadly, his parachute did not work.

Do you think it was typical?

3

HOW TO LOVE

Soon after I arrived in England I started to
work as a waitress, and I felt love every day:

'Two Fosters, my love!'

'... of course with milk, my love!'

'No, I am not talking about my penis, my love, I
am ordering a dessert. Yes, *spotted dick* is a dessert.'

I realised very soon that love (correct pronunci-
ation: 'luv') is a cheap, everyday (even more: every
minute) object in London.

English people are in love all the time and they
are not ashamed to express their love every single
opportunity they can.

English people only use the word 'love'

economically when it is about their loved one. And when I say loved one I am not talking about their pets because pets are at the same level as waitresses (maybe a little above them), which means English people can very easily express their affectionate feelings to them. It is only their actual partners that The English cannot utter the words 'I love you' to. That would be just too explicit. Sometimes, very rarely, and after a long and painful preamble they whisper into their partner's ears, 'I like you.'

But even liking their romantic partner is too outspoken for most of The English. They prefer to express their feelings mistily. Talking vaguely is as usual amongst The English as saying one thing and meaning the other, or being completely incapable of saying what they want or how they feel. Even the Spanish Inquisition would not be enough to get a true-hearted expression from The English.

So it is not a surprise if the consequence of all of these communication complications is always a disaster. A total disaster. Or better to say: a total disaster, my love.

It happened to me as well when I dated an English gentleman.

It was a Sunday afternoon and we had a stroll in Primrose Hill. It was a sunny spring day (very unusual in London) so the park was extremely busy. People were sitting everywhere on the grass, having a picnic, playing badminton, practising yoga, walking their dogs, picking up their dogs' shit with plastic gloves. It was a completely idyllic scene, perfect for life-changing moments. The view from the top of the hill was breathtaking.

My Englishman looked at me.

More precisely, he looked into my eyes. That is very un-English (English people are masters of avoiding eye contact as much as avoiding explicit talks), so I immediately had the feeling that he was going to say something very serious. And I really hoped it was not something about the weather.

He took a deep breath, gathered all his courage and confessed his feelings openly: 'I think …' (long pause) '… you are my cup of tea.'

Well, let me give you some practical advice if you don't want to commit the same mistakes I did.

First of all, never ask back furiously: 'You *think*?!?' It is a complete waste of time. It is a well-known fact that English people never *know* anything. They only *think*. The only exception they know and they are sure about in the whole world is Marmite. 'Love it or hate it.' There are no other options; there is no space for grey space.

Second, don't ask back as I did: 'Okay, thanks, I understand that I am your cup of tea, but which tea?'

To defend myself, I only asked this because I studied financial analysing, and my analytical personality always craved to understand everything in the smallest detail. And 'tea' was not detailed enough for me.

Indeed, tea is such a confusing thing in England.

English people call 'tea' not just their drink but people from the north of England call it their dinner as well. Some people call 'tea' their five o'clock tea and scone and triangle sandwich combo too.

But since he said 'cup' of tea I was sure he meant the drink, not the meal, so luckily I was already one step closer to the deeper understanding of his love.

But still I needed more information about that tea, because there are so many teas to drink!

So I kept asking:

'Am I a tea with sugar, that is to say sweet?'

'Or am I a tea with lemon, that is to say bitter?'

'Or a healthy green tea?'

'Or a tea with milk, namely eccentric?'

'Or which blend of tea?'

And where does this tea comes from? From Harrods or from Poundland? It does matter a lot, you see?

And am I the tea he desires to drink for the rest of his life or am I just an exotic tea from Hungary he just wants to taste once before returning to his national obsession: black tea with milk?

After he recovered from the minor concussion caused by all my questions he said vaguely (of course vaguely, how else?): 'I am not sure …'

Well, 'I am not sure' clearly sounded like a step back from 'I think', so I had no doubt that we were closer to the break-up than to the happily ever after. If happily ever after exists at all. I heard it does exist in certain countries, but definitely not in Hungary. Hungarian fairy tales end with '… *és boldogan éltek, amíg meg nem haltak*', in English: '… and they lived happily until they died'. As you see there is no eternal happiness for Hungarians. Death will definitely come and destroy our happiness. Maybe reincarnation would be an option but unfortunately we don't believe in that.

Finnish fairy tales end exactly the same: '… *ja he elivät onnellisina elämänsä loppuun saakka*', in

English: '… and they lived happily to the end of their lives'. Which everyone knows cannot be a long happiness as Nordic countries are number one in suicide statistics.

Romanian fairy tale ends are not optimistic either: '… *și au trăit fericiți până la adânci bătrâneți*', in English: '… and they lived happily until old age'. Sounds like it is not much fun to be old in Romania. Probably there is something wrong with the pension system. Or the health system. Or maybe Viagra is unavailable in Romania.

But Greek tale ends sound positive: '… και ζήσανε αυτοί καλά και εμείς καλύτερα', in English: '… and they lived well, and we lived better'. I would suggest updating it: '… and they lived well, and we lived better until the 2010 economic crisis'.

But Bulgarians and the Poles know how to live! (And how to drink.)

The Bulgarian happily ever after is: '… и три дни яли, пили и се веселили', which is: '… and for three days they ate, drank and had fun'.

And the Polish happily ever after: '… *a ja tam byłem, miód i wino piłem*', '… and I was there too, and drank mead and wine'.

The Spanish happy ending is all about food:

'... *y vivieron felices y comieron perdices*', '... and they lived happily and ate partridges'.

Dutch tale ends sound really surreal (after all it is the country of the free drug): '... *en toen kwam er een olifant met een lange snuit, en die blies het verhaaltje uit*', in English: '... and then came an elephant with a long snout, and it blew the story out'.

German tale ends are as rational and logical as the Germans themselves: '... *und wenn sie nicht gestorben sind, dann leben sie noch heute*', '... and if they haven't died, they are still living today'. Please note the word 'happiness' is not mentioned at all. Probably in Germany happiness is just optional.

I quite like the French ending: '... *ils vécurent heureux et eurent beaucoup d'enfants*', '... and they lived happily ever after and had many children'. Although I suspect French happiness is not about eternal children upbringing, but eternal kids making. Eternal sex.

My favourite is the Italian tale end '... *e vissero per sempre felici e contenti*', in English: '... and they were happy and content forever and ever'. Eternal happiness. That is what I want too.

But my English gentleman was clearly not

familiar with Italian, so my love story with him did not finish with eternal happiness.

Instead of responding to my fair and reasonable tea questions, he took me to his house. He went to the kitchen, put the kettle on and asked me: 'Would you like some tea?'

I said: 'No.'

Well, the only reason I just said 'No' was because, at that time, I did not know this is how most divorces in England begin and how most of the English riots, revolutions and wars start:

—*Would you like some tea?*
—*No.*

So if I can give you a lifetime advice, be always exceptionally careful with tea.

Tea is the most dangerous thing in England.

4

HOW TO LIVE WITH OTHERS

A s for many other Londoners, I couldn't afford to rent a whole house or flat from my first minimal-wage waitress salary and therefore I had to rent a room in a shared house.

I didn't just do this once. Since my debut as an alien in London, I've had the chance to share as many as eight houses! This makes me feel confident enough to tell you a little about house sharing in England.

Living in London is hugely expensive. Especially if you are miserable enough not to be anyhow related to the royal family, and have to earn your money yourself. Property prices are so ridiculously high that aliens (and lots of English people) don't dare to dream that one day they may become a property owner in London. Consequently, renting is hugely expensive and property letting is a prosperous business for the few who have houses, flats or rooms to let.

Living together with others is something that can improve your personality, reward you with lots of useful skills and eventually make you become a more open-minded alien. Which is good.

When you live with others, normally the only private place you have is your room and you have to share everything else: kitchen, bathroom and toilet, and living room (if your flat has one).

In all my house-sharing experience, sharing the kitchen always meant that all the vital space for my goods was limited to one shelf in the cupboard and one shelf in the fridge. Outside those places, my goods would have been considered as alien and therefore thrown in the bin (or rather stolen). The most obvious result is that after almost every shopping trip I realised I'd bought twice the food and drink I could safely accommodate in the limited space I had. But only until my thoughtfully precise organising skills became trained and improved.

So, thanks to my limited space in the fridge then, today I am not only the undefeated suitcase-packing champion of the world, but a Tetris master too. I can also tell you the cubic capacity of any space in less than a half second.

Sharing a kitchen and cooking with aliens from other parts of the alien world not only results in lifelong new friendships but also in new gastronomic inventions. My flatmates and I strongly believed that after political, economic and cultural globalisation it was time for culinary globalisation too. As one of the pioneers of culinary globalisation, my plan B in case I don't become a world-famous writer is to open a restaurant and share our best all-aliens-together recipes, with gourmet creations that even Jamie Oliver would envy: curry bolognese, waffle paella, kosher Frankfurter crumble, macaron burger or chocolate chip stroganoff. I must confess, my flatmates also planned to do some experimentation with our world-famous Hungarian goulash, however in that case I made it very clear that if anybody ever touched my beloved national food, I would kill that person in my next book in the worst possible way.

(Which leads to another topic: how aliens react to the 'manipulation' of their national food. The French get annoyed, Italians panic desperately, Spanish get curious, and Americans don't even realise it. But that is another story.)

One of the biggest benefits of living with other nationalities is the free language lessons. For example, I can say in more than a dozen languages 'good morning' and 'thank you' and 'you're welcome' and 'sorry' and other polite expressions. But, truth be told, every time I use these expressions during my holidays, people look at me as if I have just sworn. (Maybe I did?)

Living with others who speak different levels of English can be challenging, but this improves your skill at expressing yourself through non-verbal communication. It turns you into the absolute winner of all charade games you can enter, leaving behind even the world champion gesticulators, the Italians.

Sharing a bathroom where an entire football team has bathed before you will definitely kill your need to have a long, relaxing soak, making you realise a quick shower will suffice. A quick shower means saving time, saving money and saving water.

And this is the story of how my environmental awareness started.

In shared houses there are always at least two toilets. One of them is always typical (broken) and in the other one there is always someone reading *War and Peace* from morning to night. Bladder training doesn't sound like fun, but let's always look on the bright side: it might become a useful skill when old-age urinary incontinence decides to become part of my life.

Living with others also helped me realise how narrow-minded I was before. For example, I always used my thongs in a very old-fashioned way, as underwear. But after a couple of weeks of flat sharing, I found one of my lost thongs in my Jamaican Rasta flatmate's hair as a hair tie, a month later another was found around my Polish friend's neck, where he was using it to hold his broken elbow wrapped in plaster. Later still at our annual summer barbecue, the boys used it as a hand catapult to shoot foxes.* I felt truly honoured

* For aliens' information: The foxes in London are not escaped from the London Zoo. Thousands and thousands of foxes live in London. No, they don't look for The Little Prince, they look for food.

to live with such creative minds who are surely the greatest inventors of our generation.

Like my Turkish friend, who advised me to put a sanitary pad in my shoe when my feet were soaking wet in the rain. My first thought was as yours right now: she must be insane. But after I tried it, I realised that my friend is a genius! Because us women always have sanitary pads in our bags in case of unexpected period. But in England we can also use it for unexpected heavy rain too. After you stick it to your shoe sole, the sanitary pad absorbs all the water from your shoe and, should your sanitary pad be a luxury one with some sort of exotic scent added, it will also cover your stinky feet with its fragrance. Very glamorous. I am sure all women readers are sceptical about this idea, but if sanitary pads are soft enough for our female parts they must definitely be good enough for our feet too. Actually, this is what my French flatmate said when she used tampons as earplugs because of her new boyfriend's snoring.

Living with others helps you to understand more of the dynamics of movies. Sometimes you feel that you are in a comedy, sometimes in a working-class melodrama, occasionally in a drama, now and again a thriller (with mysterious cases such as 'who broke the cold water tap, leaving only the boiling water tap working, resulting in a quite painful hand-washing experience?'), but most of the time you feel like you are in a Latin American soap opera where time comes to a halt and the same futile conversations and arguments go on for weeks and months but nothing gets sorted, not even by the 269th episode, and you can never be sure who is your friend and who is your enemy and you just hope that the daily soap operas will never turn into a crime drama. But luckily, sooner or later, every film ends and you can start a new one. This time, hopefully, a romantic comedy with fewer supporting actors and with a true happy ending.

5

HOW TO FAKE IT IF YOU CANNOT MAKE IT

Finding a job in London is not easy. Especially if you don't speak English. That is why I started in a Turkish kebab shop. Not that I have ever spoken Turkish, but this is evidence that the 'fake it if you cannot make it' rule works brilliantly if you are brave enough. (FYI: English people use the word 'brave' as a synonym of 'crazy'.)

Then, when I finally started speaking English just as well as I spoke Turkish, I realised it was time for me to apply for a real job (by which I mean legal job), so I started to send out CVs. I was a serious CV producer, with a respectable rate of some 100

CVs per hour sent anywhere in the city. I found it more convenient to send emails than make phone calls, since in written English I sounded more fluent than vocally, and no one could pick up my distinctive Hungarian accent.

All jobseeker aliens must know that English people use understatement all the time *except* in their CV, which is total overstatement. Follow their habit, don't be ashamed to use hyperbole for your achievements.

Also, your London CV must be flexible; easily adjustable to any possible job opportunities. If you can modify your CV from barista to barrister in less than one minute then you are a proper London jobseeker.

So eventually I got it! My first (legal) job in London was being a waitress in The Narrow Boat pub and restaurant at Angel. Truth to be told, as a qualified accountant I had zero experience in the field of waitressing, also my English was still very poor. Before London, I didn't know a thing about coffee (why should I have if I don't even like coffee?), let alone coffee machines. Although my CV stated that I am a coffee expert with five years' experience I had no clue for example what a cappuccino was. One shot of coffee or two? With water or milk? Frothy milk or plain? Warm or cold?

It happened on a rainy afternoon (I am just mentioning the weather to please English readers) that the restaurant manager was at the bank, my colleague was on her break, the kitchen staff had left, and so I was alone in the whole restaurant. (It is a very English thing, closing the kitchen between 3 p.m. and 6 p.m., as if between these hours nobody ever gets hungry, right?)

Suddenly a customer came and ordered a cappuccino. My first thought was to say (accurately: lie) that the coffee machine is broken, but the poor man was dripping wet so he clearly needed a hot drink. I had no other choice than to very kindly (with my barely existent English) enquire about the nature of a cappuccino, its ingredients and recipe. Thankfully, the man was a proper English gentleman, much like Mark Darcy, exuding gentle calmness (alas, less like him in appearance). He explained everything to me in detail; what's more, he calmly stood by watching as I improvised a feat even Mr Bean would be proud of.

First, I opened the steamer without putting in the milk first and managed to burn myself. Screaming in pain, I dropped the jar of milk, drenching my clothes and the floor.

On my second attempt, I managed to heat up the milk but no froth appeared on top of it. I tried once more, but to no avail.

Then the man apologised for asking for a cappuccino.

Now this is what I call a real English politeness: apologising for ordering a cappuccino at a place where they sell cappuccino.

What's more, he came up with the idea of drinking tea instead. Moreover, he realised that he liked tea more than cappuccino.

That sounds perfect, except that I had already had trouble the day before with tea when a customer ordered an English Breakfast. How was I supposed to know that he meant the tea and not the meal they eat in the morning? Well, I should have been a bit suspicious of someone ordering breakfast after a three-course lunch, but hey, he was a customer and what I have learnt in Hungary is that customers are always right and you shall always give customers what they want, and he wanted an English Breakfast. Who was I to judge his choice? Of course he was a proper polite

English gentleman and he ate his English Breakfast without a word. Also my English manager was too polite to point out my mistake, so I only realised my mistake when my French colleague eagerly clued me in.

Knowing this, it's understandable that I got scared when Mr Cappuccino mentioned tea instead of coffee, so I rather persuaded him to let me have a last try with the cappuccino.

And finally I succeeded with the milk. Hooray!

But when I wanted to pour the milk into the cup, I couldn't hold the froth back with the spoon, so it all ended up in the middle of his coffee. Oh, not all of it, because most of it splashed out onto the bar. And onto his jacket. And his glasses.

I was really scared that he might make a scene but he didn't even say a word. Probably because he was already soaking wet by the rain so a few more drops here and there didn't really matter.

After I sprinkled his cappuccino with chocolate, I remembered him telling me that he doesn't want any chocolate on his cappuccino – so I tried to conceal my mistake with my Hollywood smile. The smile always works. Especially if I bat my eyelashes.

The gentleman smiled too. Even though he was diabetic, he wouldn't want me to start all over, he said.

When he was sitting at his table I noticed that I didn't give him a spoon or a napkin. I even forgot the biscuit that goes with a coffee. All embarrassed, I corrected my mistake.

When he finished his cappuccino (I mean stopped drinking because he left more than three-quarters of it in the cup) he left me a tip on the table that equalled the price of the coffee. I assume not because of the amazing service, but because he felt guilty for putting me in such an awkward situation. And he didn't think I would last long.

But I did last long. For years. Thanks to the English politeness.

Thank you.

6

HOW TO KEEP CALM
AND CARRY ON

KEEP CALM AND CARRY ON.

This neat little phrase invented by the British government in 1939 to motivate and comfort the population at the beginning of World War II well summarises the English way of life.

It doesn't matter if bombs are falling from the sky; you just keep calm and carry on with whatever you do.

What surprises me the most is that the British government actually never used this slogan. It seems like a war was still not enough reason for The English to worry.

Worrying is very un-English.

They say 'don't worry' nearly as frequently as they say 'sorry'. But thinking of me, how on earth should I not worry if I come from the Hungarian Republic of Worryland? And, believe me, we have had plenty of reasons to worry: we were ransacked, raped and invaded by the Mongol hordes, the Turks, the Habsburgs, the Russians and the Nazis – pretty much by everyone. So excuse me for having the Worry Genes in my DNA.

The English don't have Worry Genes in their DNA at all. Instead, they have the Keep Calm Gene.

In other countries people who bring freedom, peace or victory to their countries are the heroes. Of course these are not bad achievements in England either, but the most respected heroes are the ones who can keep themselves the calmest possible and carry on. Like the eight musicians of the *Titanic*, who played music until the very end, while the ship sank, to calm the passengers. Not all the passengers needed calming, of course, just the Americans and the other worrying aliens, since The English did not worry at all. I am sure they just drank their last stiff drink (probably a black tea) and then stood in the queue by the lifeboats, gentleman-like.

Well, what else would you call it other than heroism?

I am sure, not just us Hungarians but all the other nationalities have a lot to learn from The English in the field of keeping calm and carrying on.

There is only one tiny gap in the history of England when The English couldn't keep themselves calm. When the whole nation panicked.

No, it wasn't Blitzkrieg.

The Falklands War? Don't be ridiculous.

I will help you a little: it happened very recently.

No, not the war in Iraq and not even in Afghanistan.

Anyway, why do you think that it was a war? Bagatelle affairs like wars hardly make The English worry. It must be a far bigger event to freak them out.

I was in England at the time and I witnessed when, for the first time in history, The English couldn't keep calm and carry on. And if you think it was the 7/7 suicide bombing, you are absolutely wrong.

It was in February 2009 when a mysterious thing crippled England. The buses were removed from service; the buses, which didn't stop even during the Blitz. Trains were cancelled or were operating an emergency timetable. Thousands and thousands of

This 20cm of snow was the only episode in England's history when The English couldn't Keep Calm and Carry On.

schools were closed across England. There was chaos at all London airports, people were sleeping on the floor, waiting hours and even days for their airplane to leave. It was as if the apocalypse had come.

Half the population never made it to their workplace. And the other half who made it in were sent home as a precaution – heaven knows what might come next.

Walking to my workplace, I was listening to the radio and all channels were talking about detrimental economic impact, more than a billion pounds.

Arriving to the restaurant I realised that our chefs couldn't make it, and therefore we had no food to serve. So we were handing out yesterday's soup for free to the pedestrians who took refuge at our restaurant. They sat at the tables, staring at BBC News as if they were watching World War III live. On the TV, the transport ministry officials were trying to save their arses by telling us that 'nobody could be prepared for such chaos'.

And by chaos they meant 20cm of snow. (No, I don't have a clue how many inches that is.)

This 20cm of snow was the only episode in England's history when The English couldn't Keep Calm and Carry On.

I am sure the next one will be the global warming. And I am sure global warming will hit England just as completely unexpectedly as snow falls at winter.

7

HOW TO TALK ABOUT
THE WEATHER

WORKING AS A waitress was not the most challenging job of my life but it was the perfect place for examining The English.

Once, during a boring shift, I conducted a scientific survey amongst our customers. I was curious to know, between them ordering their drink and me serving them, how many would mention the weather in some way.

Well, not so surprisingly, twelve out of ten regulars talked about it. Yes, twelve out of ten, because two of them felt the urge to point out to me that indeed the weather changed while I was away to get their drinks. In case I hadn't noticed that the sun came out a tiny little bit but then immediately went away.

To be even more scientific, I divided the regulars from the rest. In that sample, the statistics come out at eight-and-a-half out of ten. Yes, eight-and-a-half, because there was an old chap, who, due to his mouth being full of beer, could only express his 'lovely weather today' by pointing at the sun outside.

All aliens must know that the weather-talk is the highest card in The English's deck, much like the tea, that can be used at almost any time be it noon or midnight, rain or sunshine, for better or for worse, in sickness and in health, until death takes them apart, amen.

I believe it might be useful for fellow aliens if I share my Eleven Commandments regarding the English weather:

I. In England, the weather is the main topic of conversation. English people are obsessed with the weather. Just like Germans with discipline or Italians with gestures, or we Hungarians with paprika. So be extremely careful before you open your mouth and say anything about it.

II. The weather is always mentioned in one of the following contexts:

i. To start a conversation.

ii. During a conversation, at any point when you don't know what to say. Mainly to break a silence when a topic is over. (Be prepared that there are lots of silences in English conversations.)

iii. To close a conversation.

iv Even if there's no reason to talk about the weather. Meaning: ALL THE TIME! Let's be honest, England's weather isn't worth mentioning, at all. There are no hurricanes, ice storms, heatwaves or tornadoes. It just is.

III. If someone cannot talk about the weather in long, convoluted sentences, he should expect to be labelled as a boring loser. The trump card for aliens is to say 'lovely weather today'. If you can't think of anything else, just throw this in. Even if the weather isn't lovely.

IV. Never contradict The English during weather talk. If they say that 15 degrees is 'quite unbearably hot' then either you just say that 'indeed, it is quite unbearably hot' or you just shut up and nod. (I strongly recommend to aliens the second option, because I can't picture any alien who could say the above-mentioned sentence without any hint of sarcasm in their voice.)

V. Never, and by this I mean *never*, criticise the English weather. Especially if you're an alien. For an Englishwoman, it's as though you are scolding her first-born child. For an Englishman, it's as if you are criticising the size of his penis. Or even worse: his football team.

VI. Though there's not much point in checking the BBC weather forecast (it's like reading your horoscope: what they state might happen, but actually it never does), The English are rather fond of it. If you check it more than twice a day, that's a certain sign of you turning English.

VII. England is the All-Time Champion of Rain. Though certain statistics show that Luxembourg has more, do not believe that unmitigated lie. No country has the right to claim that title from England.

VIII. In certain countries, it snows. Not in England. Not even once. Anyone who thinks that she or he ever saw snow in England must reconsider. That started out as rain but it was so cold that it froze in the meantime. But then it melted. Which proves the point: it indeed was rain.

IX. Even if you think it is hopeless, always be optimistic about the English weather. Just as optimistic as The English. The best example is the Queen's birthday. Not her actual birthday (21 April) but her official birthday. Yes, dear aliens, your best childhood dream is reality for the Queen: having two birthdays. Why? Because of the weather, of course. English people believe there is a higher possibility of nicer weather for outdoor celebrations in June than in April. But do you think that the weather is nicer on her official birthday than on her actual birthday? No, it is not. It is always typical on both days.

X. The reason that English people always talk about the weather but aliens don't is because weather talk is actually not about the weather at all. It could be any other neutral (or as The English say: 'safe') topic, and is used to avoid meaningful conversation. But the thing is that aliens don't want to avoid meaningful conversations. Aliens enjoy meaningful conversations a lot.

XI. According to English people the English weather is like a woman's mood: constantly changing and hard to predict, therefore there is always something to mention about it. That is why the weather is also the most perfect icebreaker. Aliens think that the English weather is always the same (it only changes from grey to dark grey) and they strongly believe that there is absolutely nothing to mention about it. Also, aliens don't see the necessity of an icebreaker either. Why? Because aliens are welcoming, easily approachable, unreserved and friendly people. They don't see any ice that needs to be broken at all.

8

HOW TO IMAGINE QUEUING

THERE ARE TWO kinds of people in the world. Queue lovers and queue jumpers.

It is a well-known fact that English people love queuing. George Mikes said that 'An Englishman, even if he is alone, forms an orderly queue of one.' He called queuing the English national passion.

There is only one rule in English queues, namely the FIFO rule. If you haven't studied accountancy then I will tell you what FIFO means: First In First Out.

Since they are born, every English person knows the FIFO rule and they would never under any circumstances violate this holy convention. Only aliens commit LIFO (Last In First Out) queue-jumping crimes.

You might ask what the reaction of The English is when they witness that somebody approaches the queue at any position other than the end.

The English wouldn't hesitate to shoot the queue violator immediately. But only in theory. In their sweetest dreams, every line cutter is chopped into small pieces and eaten by dogs.

But how about in practice? In real life, The English don't even dare to object. Objecting and being assertive is very un-English. They keep themselves calmer and then they just carry on standing in the queue. They might whisper to themselves that it was 'typical', but that is the farthest they can go. (Which is a typical passive-aggressive behaviour.)

In Hungary you don't find passive-aggressive people in queues. We are openly aggressive. And not just with queue jumpers but with everybody else in the queue. Standing in a queue in Hungary is like a death match. Only the strongest survive. If you reach the head of the queue without a single verbal or physical fight, that is a clear sign that the number of expats is rapidly increasing in Hungary.

But you also must know that we Hungarians have

lots of experience of standing in queues. During the socialist era, if we wanted to buy something, even basic food, we had no other choice but stand in queues for hours. For long, long hours. Sometimes even for half a day. I am sure it would have driven the passive-aggressive English aggressive too.

According to The English, the problem with queue jumpers is that they never ever experience the beauty of a queue.

A queue is like a miniature version of life itself. Even simpler than life, because you don't have to observe Ten Commandments or other laws and rules – only one, the FIFO rule. Therefore you can completely relax. You don't have to think, you don't have to make decisions, you don't have to do anything: just follow the queue. Another beauty of the queue is that everybody is equal (equality is just as important for The English as fair play); there are no HIFOs (High In First Outs), therefore the queue is like a perfect world.

I am pretty sure that queuing is what John Lennon was singing about. Just think about it …

In a queue there's no heaven, no hell below us, there are no countries, nothing to kill or die for (only Hungarians have different opinion about that). In a queue there is no religion. In a queue all the people live a life in peace. In a queue there are no possessions, no need for greed or hunger. In a queue all people share the joy of queuing.

You may say English people are dreamers, but they hope someday all aliens will join them in the queue and the world will live as one.

Amen to that.

9

HOW TO MIND YOUR OWN BUSINESS

ENGLISH PEOPLE ARE very reserved. And they don't like it if other people don't respect their privacy.

I learnt this rule in a hard way. Really hard.

After one-and-a-half years of waitressing, my dream came true when I was offered an office intern job while cleaning tables. If in the restaurant all my colleagues were aliens, in the office I found myself working mostly with English people. Making no difference for me, I initially approached them in the same friendly way as I was used to do with my former alien colleagues, but then I realised that every time I dared to ask something, apart from 'How are you?', I had the strong feeling that they interpreted it as if I wanted to steal their bank card PIN. (Or even worst: their social media password.) Since expressing feelings and thoughts is very un-English, of course, they refrained from saying anything, but the expression of their faces was pretty clear: 'Would you please mind your own business?' Now, before you think that probably I asked something too personal, like their penis/bra sizes, let me confess that I simply asked them a question like 'Which way are you going?' when we left the office.

To my big surprise, The English do not want you to know in which direction they are travelling. Sometimes English people ask you which way you are going. But don't be flattered, they ask it not because they want to join you; they just want to make sure which direction they shouldn't choose, under any circumstances.

I got the same reaction when I asked if they had any plans for the weekend. They always said 'no, not really' or 'nothing much'. Even if I heard them on the phone, five minutes later, saying they are organising a huge BBQ party for the weekend or they are going to a wedding. I guess they'd say the same 'nothing much' response even if it was going to be their own wedding.

Likewise, I felt rejection when I asked their opinion about something. According to The English, everything is nice. The weather (of course). My new dress. My genuine Hungarian goulash. My bum (which is, let's be honest, rather concave than convex). Therefore aliens tend to think that English people are undereducated and they didn't learn any other word apart from nice. The truth is that they know thousands and thousands of other words too but sharing their intimate thoughts and feelings about something means violating their own privacy. That is why they use *nice* all the time. Because *nice* is shallow. Because *nice* is safe. Because *nice* is nice.

What surprises me the most is that even if you wish something to The English, they will look at you with the mind-your-own-business expression on their faces. For example wishing them, 'Have a nice day', which I learnt from my former alien colleagues at the restaurant (who definitely didn't learn British but American English at school in their homeland). The English do not like to be wished 'have a nice day' because to them it sounds like a command. They think, who the hell do you think you are to order them to have a nice day? They will have a nice day if they feel like having a nice day, it's their own choice. Maybe they had a nice day yesterday, and the day before too, and today finally they want to have their 'typical' English day.

Also, you have to know that The English, more often than not, are sarcastic. Therefore if you wish them 'have a nice day' they tend to think that you are just being sarcastic. And that is probably why they don't even bother to respond.

Another example: English people don't like to be told 'enjoy your meal'. They will enjoy their meal if they feel like enjoying it. It is advisable not to command them such things in case they have other plans with their meal, such as preferring to dislike it.

English people have the absolute right to dislike whatever they want, anytime they want.

That is why The English don't like marketing because advertisements tell them what to like. The English don't like to be advised what deodorant or car they should like and buy. They like to decide on their own without any influence. In *How to be Inimitable*, George Mikes wrote it would be advisable to approach The English with modest advertisements like 'GRAPIREX: It may relieve your headache. Or, of course, it may not. Who can tell? Try it. You may be lucky. The odds against you are only 3 to 1' or 'S.O.S. We are doing badly. Business is rotten. Buy Edgeless Razor Blades and give us a sporting chance. Honestly, they're not much worse than other makes.'

Thanks George, this is the best advice ever! And not just on how to approach The English in terms of marketing but also on how to approach them in everyday life.

So I changed my strategy.

Instead of asking them 'Which way are you going?' when we leave the office I just tell them, 'I am going this way. Please don't hesitate to join me if you feel the slightest chance that my alien companionship might not bore you to death.'

Or instead of wishing them 'Have a nice day' I just say, 'It doesn't look a horrible day, the kind of day perfect for your suicide, so please feel free to enjoy it if it is not against your original intention.'

And instead of saying 'Enjoy your meal' I simply say, 'Your meal doesn't look that bad, you might survive eating it. Best of luck!'

Since then, they always say that I am funny. And I always respond, 'Please don't refrain yourself from being sarcastic any time you feel its necessity.'

10

HOW NOT TO USE A HOT-WATER BOTTLE

Ｉ COME FROM A small village, with a population of 1,000 people, in a remote corner of southern Hungary. I am not saying that I grew up with archaic morals, but yes, compared to my London friends my sexual education was clearly behind the times.

In George Mikes' book there's a chapter on sex which reads: 'Continental people have sex lives; the English have hot-water bottles.' Nothing else, the whole chapter is just that plain, simple, concise and inspiring phrase.

'Hmm ...' I thought when I read it 'Hot-water bottle? Probably it is some sort of a sex toy, and George was too prudish to talk more about it.'

And that was it. I didn't pay any more attention to that hot-water bottle, something that was (and still is) completely unknown in my thousand-people village.

It came to my mind again only when my boyfriend broke up with me and I needed some ... well ... you know what. (As you see when it comes to sex talking I can be more English than The English themselves.)

Anyway, a hot-water bottle seemed as a solution worth to give a try. I thought it might even help me to understand The English more through their sexual habits.

In John Lewis, I must say I was a little shocked when I found the hot-water bottles.

I am not sure what was I expecting, but definitely something else. First of all, something smaller.

Some of them looked really kinky. Especially the 'John Lewis Brown Shaggy Dog Hot-Water Bottle'. I definitely didn't need that shag.

Finally I chose one: a simple grey fur without any recognisable animal personality. (I know what you're thinking: what an old-fashioned woman I am.)

I paid for it, left the shop quickly and rushed home.

I was really looking forward to enjoying my first sex toy.

I locked my room, took out my sex toy from the shopping bag and started to read the instructions carefully.

Unfortunately there wasn't detailed enough directions for use, so I didn't really get how it could have given me an orgasm. But anyway I followed the steps and filled it up with hot but not boiling water and closed it carefully.

I was a little concerned about what kind of interaction I could expect between the grey fur filled with hot water and my female parts, but I was aware of English people's health and safety obsession so I thought even if the sexual act goes wrong I would probably not damage myself too much. The English don't look like the kind of people whose sexual enjoyment includes lifetime health damages.

So I went to bed, took off my panties and … well … I waited.

And waited.

And waited.

But nothing happened.

(I know what you are thinking now, but in the end, the hot-water bottle did provide an orgasm, so keep reading.)

After a while I got bored of waiting and waiting and waiting, and so I checked the instructions again. There were still no further steps!

I read George's chapter about sex again but I didn't find any hidden advice between the lines.

I was completely lost. How should I approach my sex toy? Should I fondle or caress it?

Logic said that fondling or caressing could not be the key to making it work, since English people hardly fondle and caress anyone apart from their pets. So what else? Should I follow the English etiquette and offer it a cup of tea?

I was really desperate. But if anything, at least it was warm. And if I became thirsty I could drink from it. Probably English people put tea in it and the Russians vodka instead of tap water. Another advantage I found during waiting was that it could not make women pregnant.

I fell asleep unsatisfied, thinking that, the next day, I would ask my colleagues how to use it properly. I was sure it would be hard to bring up such a juicy subject between two 'lovely weather today' conversations, but I would have to give it a try.

At dawn, half asleep, I turned around in my bed and I felt something unusual. First, still half asleep, I touched it with my feet and I felt something furry. Also I felt as something was moving. Still half asleep I looked under my duvet and …

… according to my flatmate she heard a big scream and she ran into my room (but first she had to break my door, because I locked it to have privacy with my sex toy), and there she found me screaming hysterically and crying.

My flatmate shook me really hard a couple of times before I could speak and tell her that there was a dead rat in my bed!

She didn't believe me, of course.

So, she took my umbrella, lifted up my duvet and poked the rat with the umbrella.

After she stopped screaming she confirmed that it was indeed a dying rat.

Evidence number one: it had a grey fur.

Evidence number two: when she poked its belly with the umbrella she felt its softness.

None of us had heart (more precisely: guts) to beat the rat to death with my umbrella, so we decided that we should find a man to do the dirty job.

On the floor below us lived a Spanish couple, a Russian guy and a French chap.

My flatmate volunteered to knock on the Russian guy's door and ask for his help. He looked more hero type than the French bloke. (No offence.)

Mr Russia happily came upstairs. (Of course, because my Brazilian flatmate was the beauty itself, she could have easily charm any man to any war.)

We were waiting in the kitchen while Mr Hero went into my room. He said he didn't need my umbrella. (Miss Brazil said that this is what she calls a *real man*.)

No more than couple of seconds later, Mr Rat-Killer was standing in the kitchen door with my sex toy in his hand, looking at us suspiciously, clearly waiting for an explanation.

I never felt so embarrassed in my whole life.

I didn't know what to say. (And this time not because of my poor English.) Mr Russia didn't seemed to mind the long silence, because he discovered my flatmate's boobs under her nightdress. So

I took advantage of his distraction and quickly left the scene.

Then, a little later I heard some easily identifiable noises. It wasn't loud, but since I had no door anymore I could hear all the moans and suppressed screams.

So, I concluded, they must have figured out how The English use hot-water bottles to fulfil their sexual lives.

11

HOW NOT TO LOSE YOUR SUPERPOWER

I HAVE ALWAYS BEEN a dreamer.

When I was a little girl I used to daydream about having a superpower. When I was late from school I used to wish I had Flash's superhuman speed. When I forgot to do my homework I used to wish for Professor X's memory manipulation, so I could erase the homework from my teacher's memory. When my teacher locked me in the classroom all afternoon because of my missing homework I used to daydream about having Superman's flight ability. And when my fly away from the classroom did not end with success and I ended up in hospital,

I dreamed about owning Wolverine's ability to be healed immediately from my injury.

Since then I grew up, and of course I don't dream about superpowers anymore.

All right, I confess, since I moved to England sometimes I dream about Storm's superhuman ability. It would be quite useful to be able to control the English weather from grey and dark grey to bright and sunny. But now I am not here to talk about the weather. I am here to talk about the English superpower. Yes, there is an English superpower.

And if you haven't caught sight of their superhuman ability yet it could only mean one thing: they are absolutely masters of their superpower.

Invisibility.

English people love being invisible.

That is why they hide behind newspapers and make-up mirrors on the tube, that is why they wear big sunglasses in a country where there is hardly any sunshine and that is why they pretend they are fiercely answering important text messages every morning when they spot an acquaintance standing at the same platform. When the acquaintance unmasks their invisibility (only aliens do such a graceless thing, The English highly respect each other's invisibility), from that day English people would rather wake up every single morning half an hour earlier just to take the earlier train and avoid the person who has seen through their invisibility.

Nothing horrifies The English more than when someone unveils their invisibility. Believe me, I once witnessed a situation when the English invisible superpower was unmasked.

It was truly a lifetime experience for me.

Once upon a time I dated an Englishman. We planned to cook *pasta al pesto* for dinner but we did not have pesto at home, so we went to the local Sainsbury's. The pesto was on sale – buy one get one free – so we bought two.

When we headed to the cashier my Englishman started to behave very awkwardly. First, he slowed down, and then suddenly he changed his direction.

'Where are you going?' I asked him.

'To look around.'

'To look around?! You hate looking around!'

'Who told you that?'

'You!'

'Well, I might make an exception today.'

'Why?'

'There is no particular reason, I just feel like it.'

'Look, I am really hungry! Can we please go home?'

'All right, but can you please wait a little?'

'Wait for what?'

'Wait until my neighbour leaves. I spotted him earlier. I think it was him.'

'Do you just think or are you sure? Anyway what is wrong with your neighbour?'

'Nothing.'

'Then why don't you want to meet him?'

'No reason in particular. I just don't want to meet him.'

'But *why*?'

'Because I don't want to talk to him.'

'Why not? I thought you English love small-talk talks.'

'No, we hate it!'

'Really?! You English are the masters of small talk.'

'Yes. But only because we hate big talks even more.'

'Are you saying that you prefer to hide behind the baked beans just to avoid small talk with a man who might be your neighbour but maybe he isn't?'

'Jesus! You foreigners are such …'

'Are you saying that you prefer to hide behind the baked beans just to avoid small talk with a man who might be your neighbour but maybe he isn't?'

'Oh, I see, so he is a foreigner, that is why you don't like him?'

'No, actually I was talking about you. He is English.'

'Well, if he is English too, there is no need for you to worry about meeting him because probably he is playing exactly the same invisible secret agent game as you.'

'You think so?'

'*Yes!* So, can we please go to the cashier now?'

'All right. But hold on, definitely not that way!'

'Why not? The cashiers are there!'

'I know, but if we go that way ...'

'You mean the shortest way?'

'... then he will have a chance to see what is in our basket.'

'Why? There is nothing in our basket apart from the pesto. Unless you bought an invisible suicide bomb.'

'Don't be ridiculous!'

'Of course, *I* am being ridiculous. All right, then tell me what the hell is wrong with our pesto?'

(To be honest, I did not say 'what the hell'. I said something else.)

'There is nothing wrong with pesto. But they are on buy one get one free sale.'

'So?'

'It looks like I came here just because of the pesto sale. I don't want him to think that I have financial difficulties. It is already a shame that he saw me in Sainsbury's and not in Marks and Spencer.'

'Do you think he cares about you in that detail?'

(Again, this is not literally what I asked.)

'All right, maybe he doesn't, but let's not risk it.'

(Yes, this is what he literally said: 'let's not *risk* it'. As you see English people are not very adventurous, they prefer to avoid all sorts of risks.)

So we bought a couple of other things (that we didn't need at all) and then we headed to the cashier. (Of course he chose the longest and most complicated way to the cashier a human being could possibly choose. Once I even thought we were lost.)

Finally, we were standing in the queue and his neighbour (it was definitely him, my Englishman confirmed) was standing in the other queue (of course the farthest he could choose from us) when his cashier suddenly closed her till and asked him to move to the shortest queue, which was our queue.

Believe me, the tension of the Cold War was nothing compared to the tension between these two

English neighbours. They were both scared to death that their invisible superpower would perish.

I was ready for everything.

And when I say everything I mean *absolutely everything*.

There was a big leek in the other guy's basket and I am sure he would rather stab himself death with the leek than become visible to us. But it was too late for such braveness; he had to stand behind us.

I assume you will not believe me, but I swear, this is exactly what happened. It was the most interesting, instructive and thought-provoking conversation I ever witnessed:

'Hi. How are you?'

'Good, thank you. And you?'

'Good.'

End of conversation.

12

HOW TO BLAME

THE ENGLISH LOVE blaming themselves.

Whatever the situation, they say 'I'm sorry, my mistake' without even thinking. A proper Englishman is so cheeky that he tries to claim the blame every single time. Last week I witnessed two of my English colleagues getting into a quarrel over whose fault it was that a mug of tea got spilled.

'Oh, I'm sorry, my fault.'

'No, it's my fault.'

'No, it's mine!'

'Absolutely not, it's mine!'

They almost got into a fight.

I also witnessed two alien chaps get into a similar fight – except that in their case the argument was like this:

'It's your fault, not mine!'

'What? You screwed up, it's your fault!'

'How dare you! We both know you screwed up!'

'Liar! You're a liar!'

If we take the courage and dare to examine the two scenes above we can clearly see the main difference between The English and the aliens. (I can already tell you it is not a typo that I always use initial caps for The English, but small letter for aliens.)

Here it is:

The aliens think they are perfect; they never make mistakes. Not even once. It follows that if someone tries to unmask their imperfections, to dare to say that they made a mistake (such as spilling a cup of tea), this someone must be aware that they risk their life.

But what about The English?

The English don't *think* they are perfect. The English *know* they are. (Apart from Marmite this is the only thing they are sure about.)

Now, you may ask how admitting to mistakes fits in with perfectness.

Well, here comes the twist which reveals the complicated labyrinth of The English person's soul: The English are fed up with being perfect.

Being perfect all the time is just the pain in the neck, isn't it?

So that is why The English admit to mistakes constantly. Of course, don't be naive – The English never spill tea by accident, just as colonising half of the world wasn't merely a fatal accident either. Not at all. The English are too perfect to make mistakes by accident, only aliens make such serious errors.

But it is really not The English's fault that they are perfect, so we don't have the right to be resentful. It is quite enough a curse for them. Because it doesn't matter how many or how big mistakes The English make, they can never be more imperfect than the most perfect alien.

And this guilty feeling of perfection is the reason why The English blame themselves, all the time regardless of who made the mistake.

I guess you want to know how the quarrels ended.

I will start with the two aliens' disagreement since it was way simpler. I just dialled 999. One of them left the crime scene in a police car, the other one in an ambulance.

But the disagreement between the two Englishmen did not end that easily. Because both of them were gentlemen. And an English gentleman never under any circumstances hits someone who is weaker than him. And of course both of them were sure that they had the dominant position. In which position even such unmitigated lie as someone daring to claim that the spilled tea on the kitchen floor was his fault was still not enough reason for an Englishman to commit violence.

I assume now you understand how serious the situation was. I had to outsmart two Englishmen at the same time.

Finally, very cunningly I said that the spilled tea wasn't either of their faults, but mine.

I only dared to say such thing because I was sure they both were gentlemen so they will not strike me dead immediately.

Of course they were not satisfied with my answer. I had to support my statement with more evidence than simple take the blame.

The basis of my pleading speech was the fact that it all happened on Thursday. It is a well-known fact that English office workers don't greet daily, but weekly. To those silly ones who doesn't know this rule (to fellow aliens) I will explain: The English greet you with 'Good morning' on Monday morning and say goodbye with 'Have a nice weekend' on Friday afternoon before they leave the office, and in between they only combine 'how are you?' and 'lovely weather today' and 'would you like a cup of tea?' and 'hi'. (FYI: the 'hi' is more like just hemming than a clear 'hi'.)

The ominous tea spill incident happened on a Thursday morning. Consequently, in my English colleagues' eyes my 'good morning' greeting was completely unnecessary. In fact so unnecessary that both of them were so shocked that they forgot the tea and looked at me like they were seeing a ghost. Jack was holding the kettle, John was holding the two mugs, and the tea was just all over the kitchen floor.

Finally, they agreed that *maybe* it was my fault, *maybe* my greeting confused them. (FYI: Never to be sure and always being vague is a typical English thing. They never say a clear 'yes' or 'no'; it is like these two words are swear words. The most you can achieve is a 'maybe'.)

Luckily they forgave me for my unnecessary greeting, but only because I am an alien and therefore unable to understand their extremely difficult greeting rules.

Do you want to know why blaming myself was the quickest way to silence the disagreement? Because blaming myself is one of the most obvious signs that I was trying to become English. Of course, The English's opinion is that I have way more chance of becoming an orangutan than English, but The English are exceptional polite folks, so even if they know I have zero chance of succeeding they will let me try. The elephants in the circus who try to sit like human beings also amuse The English very much, so why shouldn't they let themselves be amused by my attempt to become English with my poor blaming-myself trick? According to them, everyone wants to be English. Being English is the best thing in the world. (Far behind, the second best thing is being God himself.)

After we closed the case I wiped up the evidence from the kitchen floor and they put the kettle on again.

The next day I found two letters on my desk. One from the United Nations asking my advice about the Middle East war, the other one from Norway, announcing that I was nominated to the Nobel Peace Prize.

13

HOW TO KISS IN THE RAIN

CONSIDERING HOW RAINY England is, statistically it should be the worldwide champion of kissing in the rain.

But has Miss Kiss ever seen any English people kissing in the rain?

Nope, I haven't.

There are countries where public affection is not tolerated, in certain countries it is even forbidden, considered a violation of law and punished with a fine or imprisonment. I investigated scrupulously the English law, so you can believe me when I say that England doesn't belong to those countries where public affection is a criminal offence.

So why don't The English kiss in the rain?

I spent a good many years running a survey and asking English people about it. Please find here all the reasons they said:

Reason number one: health.

In England everything is a health and safety issue. Exchanging saliva already brings a certain health risk, but kissing a person who might already have a cold or flu because of the rain, or catching cold and flu while kissing in the rain, is definitely a double risk.

Of course there are exceptions. There are English who are more passionate than health-concerned, but their passion comes either from their secretly well-hidden alien birth certificate or from alcohol.

Reason number two: safety.

Since nobody shows public affection in England, if an English couple kissed in the rain everybody would focus on them, pedestrians, car drivers, bus drivers, even pilots from the sky, and that would result in mass accidents all over the country.

Also, kissing in the rain could be dangerous not just for bystanders but also for the kissing couple itself. First of all, if it rains the pavement can be slippery. If one of them slips more likely the other one will slip too and both of them will end up on the pavement badly injured, with bleeding bitten-off tongues.

A bitten-off tongue can also happen if someone bumps into the kissing couple and pushes them.

Also, English people think it is possible to drown while kissing in the rain, since your mouth is open collecting all that water.

So as you see kissing in the rain is a highly dangerous business. Only the bravest should try.

Reason number three: Hollywood.

There are certain things that English people find quite entertaining on screen but not in their life. Like disaster or horror movies. They very much enjoy watching them with salt and vinegar crisps and a cup of tea but they would never volunteer to be part of any real disaster or horror. Kissing in the rain belongs to this category too.

Waiting to be kissed in the rain is only excusable if you have a ginger cat in your arms and you stroke it with eyes filled with tears. But then you have to resemble Audrey Hepburn. More precisely, you actually have to be her. There are no other excuses for kissing in the rain. In Hollywood rain and kiss are directly proportional: the more it rains the more chance you have to see a kissing scene soon. In

England rain and kiss are inversely proportional. You may ask why. Because English people are eccentric, they like inverse things. The best example is that they drive on the left-hand side of the road.

Reason number four: umbrella.

Much like we pessimist Hungarians always see the worst coming, The English always see the rain coming. It means they always carry an umbrella. Always.

But how should they kiss in the rain with umbrellas? Should the umbrellas be closed or open? Kissing in the rain, soaking wet, with closed umbrellas in their hands? English people are eccentric but not that much. But if they both open their umbrellas they could easily stab each other's eyes with them and then we are back to the good old health and safety issue again. As you see umbrellas are considered as dangerous weapons in England.

Reason number five: morals.

In the mind of The English, kissing in the rain, as well as other public displays of affection, belongs to the category of soft porn. Sane people don't do soft porn in public. Only animals do. And aliens.

English people are reserved. They do such bad things only at home. That's why, if it rains, you see all The English running faster than running the London Marathon. They enthusiastically rush home and into their back garden and start kissing passionately in the rain.

Or so I've been told.

14

HOW ENGLISH HUMOUR
DOESN'T EXIST

THE ENGLISH ARE exceptionally proud and fond of their humour. They state it is unique, the best in the world, or even the entire universe. Furthermore, according to The English, their humour is simply unintelligible to aliens.

George Mikes was an ideal candidate to accept this challenge. First of all because he was a humourist, secondly because he was an alien. Although he became a British citizen in 1946 when his book *How to be an Alien* was published, he said: 'A criminal may improve and become a decent member of society. A foreigner cannot improve.

Once a foreigner, always a foreigner. There is no way out for him. He may become British, he can never become English.'

George Mikes scrupulously examined the English humour. He even wrote a book about it: *English Humour for Beginners*; and its first sentence is: 'English Humour resembles the Loch Ness Monster in that both are famous but there is a strong suspicion that neither of them exist.'

After I read his book I decided that I too should challenge myself in the quest for English humour. Now I know that finding the Loch Ness Monster would have been far easier.

The purpose of humour (at least in alien countries) is to laugh and to make laugh. But not in England. Laughing is absolutely un-English.

English humour must be delivered deadpan, and it must be accepted by the English audience with a complete straight face. This results in a total confusion for aliens. Total confusion is still not enough to satisfy The English, so they throw their favourite 'I'm just kidding' phrase on the top of it. But unlike aliens, English people say 'I'm just kidding' if they are kidding but also if they are not kidding at all. And when poor aliens dare to ask whether The English were really kidding or not, that is when The English smile satisfied and say 'You know what I mean?' and leave the scene. That is so typical of them, and of course aliens don't have a slightest clue at all about what The English meant or where the humour was.

Having been through this (embarrassing) situation a lot, and feeling that I didn't have any sense of humour at all, I started to suspect that the primary purpose of English humour is not the humour itself but to confuse aliens. Just as cockney people developed their rhyming slang to confuse non-locals and police officers.

Think about it. The English language is spoken by billions throughout the world. For The English, this is an advantage because wherever they go they will always be understood. But it can be a disadvantage too, for exactly the same reason: English people don't have the freedom to talk about their wild sex life or their secretly invented home-made Worcester sauce recipe whenever they feel like it, because not just The English but also all the aliens can understand them. As opposed to, for example, my language, which is only spoken in Hungary and is so unique that it was used as a military code during the American Civil War.

So, just as the Hungarian language was used as a code, or as cockney people developed rhyming slang, in exactly the same way The English invented English humour as their foreign language in order to puzzle aliens.

And I am telling you they did a pretty good job, because English humour always was and still is an enigma for foreigners. A far bigger mystery than the Loch Ness Monster.

Here is my advice to aliens on how to successfully employ English humour in their life (be careful, it only works on other aliens, never on English people):

If you happen to say or do something extremely embarrassing that will disgrace you for the rest of your life (such as confessing that you are a serious serial spoon-kleptomaniac who steals spoons not only from cafés and restaurants but also from office meeting refreshment trays and friends' homes, to save your neck you should immediately say confidently: 'Hey, it was English humour!' If you want to make it really effective, you can add a hint of disappointment in your audience for not catching it in the first instance. Since other aliens don't have a clue what English humour is, instead of stigmatising you for your craziness they will immediately forgive you and laugh out loud. Of course, it will be a forced laugh, since nobody knows what they are laughing about. Since somehow I am master of embarrassing myself accidentally, I have used this technique several times: it is good fun; all aliens should try it once. At least you will understand how satisfied English people feel when they confuse aliens with their English humour.

I didn't finished George Mikes' quotation from the beginning of this chapter. It goes: 'English Humour resembles the Loch Ness Monster in that both are famous but there is a strong suspicion that neither of them exist. Here the similarity ends: the Loch Ness Monster seems to be a gentle beast and harms no one; English Humour is cruel.'

15

HOW TO WORK

ENGLISH PEOPLE LOVE working.

If it is about their job they are exceptionally hard-working and terrifically enthusiastic. One and all.

I know what you are thinking: 'Bollocks!'

But please, don't rush to such a conclusion; don't judge them simply on what you see on the surface. Because on a daily basis, yes, English people might not seem to be the world's most hard-working nation, but have you ever thought why?

George Mikes had his answer: 'They just don't like hard work. The Germans have a reputation for hard work, so they like to keep it up. The British find it boring.'

Well, in this case, I must contradict George.

My theory is that English people love hard work. But it is our fault, the aliens' fault, that English people don't work hard. The last thing The English want is to embarrass us aliens with the unrivalled diligent English work ethic. Fair play is above everything else. And that is why English people play the lazy employee, with complete apathy and passivity all the time: to give a chance to us aliens to succeed. Fair play strictly dictates that they don't take themselves or their jobs too seriously, they must let aliens play a bit of the working game too. Even more: let aliens work harder, so they will not feel discriminated against.

The only thing English people take seriously at their workplaces is the breaks: tea breaks (every two hours) and lunch breaks (twice a day, if possible). If The English have a chance to choose their place at work they choose the closest to the kitchen, more precisely to the kettle, since for them there is nothing more relaxing during work than hearing the boiling kettle next door. And you can believe me, in English offices kettles are filled to the top and hissing impatiently all the time. Being polite and leaving water in the kettle for the next colleague (who will reboil it anyway) is far more important than saving energy, saving money or indeed saving our planet.

The English's other favourite place at work is the closest to the exit. At lunchtime or at the end of the day they prefer to leave the office as soon as they can and the quickest they can (which is also useful to play the invisible game, since in such a way they significantly reduce the chances of bumping into a colleague leaving the office, forcing them to comment on the weather they are going to find outside).

English politeness is deeply burnt in their DNA, so at lunchtime they always ask their colleagues if anyone want to join them. However you can clearly see the big relief on their face when everybody remain silent. But I am telling you; the truth is that they are not going out to have lunch. I mean, yes, they always come back with food, but for The English the main point of the lunchtime is not the food itself. Aliens like to go out at lunchtime to relax in parks, or walk, or go to massage or yoga or to the gym – for English people, the most efficient source of relaxation is stand in a queue and wait for a triangle sandwich, stand in a queue and wait for a salt and vinegar crisps and stand in a queue and wait for a tea.

Another workplace activity English people like more than their actual job is flirting during working hours. If it is about the flirt, their favourite 'work hard, play hard' motto applies. They play the flirt game really, really hard. This is one of the rare fields of their life where fair play doesn't apply. But the intensity of the flirting is strictly inversely proportional: the less they like the person the more courage with which they flirt. So if your English colleague never flirts with you, there is a big possibility that he or she is truly madly deeply in love with you secretly.

All these hidden feelings of English employees will come to surface at the company's Christmas party. This is the only time when they lose control (after couple of stiff drinks paid by the company) and then friendships and all other sort of relationships are born easily between people who, apart from work and weather-related issues, have never discussed anything before. Stiff English bodies that were completely incapable of dancing a couple of minutes earlier fill the dance floor with all sorts of performances. (Dance category: drunken, subcategory: freestyle, genre: total embarrassment.) The bravest English even dare to do things that only aliens do: they look into their dance partner's eyes and smile.

The whole office Christmas party is like a carnival. More precisely like an inverse carnival, because The English don't put masks on to pretend to be someone else but they take off their mask and allow themselves to be actually themselves. And, to their biggest surprise, they realise that their colleagues are not that bad. They are friendly, likeable and interesting people with whom they might even enjoy socialising outside work.

Then, when all the alcohol is gone and all the repressed feelings are confessed, English colleagues say goodbye to each other and go home. For the first time in their lives they go home together and on the way home they cheerfully realise how close they live to each other: the next street or even next door. But just as magic only lasts until midnight in fairy tales, the cheerfulness of The English about living close to each other doesn't last long either.

The very next working day, everybody goes back to the invisible game. Everybody puts their formal mask on and do the walk of shame as if the Christmas party was just a one-night stand they are terribly embarrassed by.

After the first awkward working day everything goes back to normal. By normal I mean 'typical', of course.

16

HOW TO BE POLITE

ENGLAND IS THE land of politeness. Politeness above all.

However, if it is about politeness, English people believe in quantity rather than quality. For example: sorry. Aliens say sorry very rarely, but if they do, they absolutely mean it from the bottom of their heart. English people say sorry all the time without any meaning, even when they haven't caused the incident which the apologies are for. 'Sorry', for The English, is just another conditioned reflex, like when you press the belly of those talking puppets to make them recite the pre-recorded phrase.

My favourite 'sorry' is when English people apologise for something that has not even happened yet. A typical example is when you get to a door at the same time as an Englishman. You can bet the Englishman will stop immediately and start apologising, as if the two of you already got stuck within the door frame so badly that even a one-week effort of all London's firefighters couldn't rescue you, and it was all his fault, of course.

My other favourite is the 'bumping-into-some-one-sorry'. It doesn't matter who bumps who (or just nearly bumps): they will say sorry automatically. As I said, it's like when you press the puppet's belly. They're so fast with their 'sorry' that an alien simply has no chance to apologise first. Seriously. I even tested it by bumping into English people deliberately, just to discover I never managed to say sorry first.

The most extraordinary English politeness I ever witnessed was when a Latin American boy stepped into our overcrowded tube carriage. He had a rucksack on his shoulders and a 'baby on board' sign on his jacket. Yes, he was a teenage boy with a pregnant badge. Everybody looked at him suspiciously; also people were looking at each other confused. Then, finally, an English gentleman politely stood up and gave his seat to the boy with a well-mannered smile (instead of saying: Look, you are a man, and men cannot be pregnant! Take that bloody badge off and bugger off!).

George Mikes said: 'In England it is bad manners to be clever, to assert something confidently. It may be your own personal view that two and two make four, but you must not state it in a self-assured way, because this is a democratic country and others may be of a different opinion.'

That Latino boy clearly had a different opinion about pregnancy and The English let him have it. This incident is a good example of pointing out that we aliens have a lot to learn, but I am still not sure it is a lesson about English politeness or Latin American smartness.

Another example of English politeness is the 'how are you?' English people ask 'how are you?' more often than anything else. If, being in England, you don't ask that question at least 5.5 times per hour, you are clearly an alien. (The .5 is for when you only raise your eyebrows.) For aliens' information, this question is just a compulsory kindness, not meant to be taken seriously. In Hungary, you only ask 'how are you?' when you are honestly interested in the answer and have a lot of time for a long response which always involves the price of petrol, some health problems and some corrupt politician. In England, people will barely listen for the answer. In Hungary, this is the question to be avoided at all costs; in England, it is the answer that is avoided. Like at the best philosophical debates, what matters is the question, never the answer. (So English people are not only polite but also deeply philosophical.)

If an Englishman asks you 'how are you?', they only expect two possible answers: 'not bad' and 'not too bad'. The former means 'I am doing great', the latter that you are about to commit suicide or have some terminal disease. With anything else, you risk being tarred and feathered. Also, if your answer is 'excellent' they take it as sarcasm.

Same quantity vs quality rule applies to the 'are you okay?' question. In England, if you express the faintest sign of unhappiness, people will ask you if you're all right. Sometimes even between strangers. The only acceptable answer is 'yes, I'm fine'. However, I also experienced some quality politeness I want to share with you, just to be fair.

On my first week in England, a homeless beggar asked me if I was all right. (I wasn't all right at all. I didn't speak English, I didn't have a job and I wasn't even sure what the hell I was doing in England.)

On my first week in England, a homeless beggar asked me if I was all right. (I wasn't all right at all. I didn't speak English, I didn't have a job and I wasn't even sure what the hell I was doing in England.) And that beggar's question made me think a lot. And not only about how shameful it was to be in a situation where a homeless beggar was worrying about me, but, again, about English politeness: if someone from the lowest possible level of the world-renowned English class system is that polite, well that tells a lot about English politeness.

The last time I exchanged words with a homeless person was back in Hungary, he said to me: 'Hey honey, can I have a shag instead of your money?'

So how did I reply to the English beggar? I wanted to give him some coins but he shook his head kindly, smiling at me (probably he sensed that I needed that money more than him), and wished me good luck before I left. I needed luck, a lot. I stood up from the bench I was sitting on and crying and I entered the building where my first English job interview was. (Yes, without speaking English. It is very common among us aliens.)

Since then, any time I observe reflex politeness in England, I think of that beggar, who proved that there are exceptions. Indeed, there are English people who care about others not by reflex but from the heart.

17

HOW TO INTERPRET THE
ENGLISH LANGUAGE

ENGLISH COMMUNICATION IS extremely indirect. As a result, if you want to understand what someone means you must learn to read between the lines, from right to left and from bottom to top.

For me it was really hard to understand this since Hungarian communication is completely the opposite. In Hungary people always say what they think without hesitation. However, it has not always been like that. There was a time when Hungarians were not allowed to say all they wanted. Or, more precisely, they were but then they had to bear the consequences: life or death sort of consequences ruled out by the political police. It was not so long ago, during and after World War II when we became an oppressed nation.

Understandably, after our oppressors left our country and freedom of speech was restored, Hungarians could freely and explicitly say what they liked. And they have kept doing it all the time since then.

Freedom of speech is like chocolate. If, as a kid, you were allowed to eat as many chocolates as you wanted, chocolate will never be of value to you. But if, as a kid, chocolate was forbidden, eventually you will see it as invaluable. So precious, that you will even steal a chocolate without caring about the consequences. And later, when you become adult, and chocolate is there for you all the time, you will devour it for breakfast, lunch and dinner, until you are sick.

To help aliens understand the labyrinth of English communication, here is an alien translation of some of the phrases you most frequently come across in English professional life.

English people say:
This is our new colleague, Tim. Let's introduce ourselves.

Translation:

Hey, a new human being to interact with. I've already spoken about the weather and he already had his tea. So let's make this quick and get back to the invisible game.

English people say:

Thanks for your CV. I will file it.

Translation:

It's time for paper shredding.

English people say:

That is quite an unusual business suggestion.

Translation:

Can someone please call the mental hospital?

English people say:

Everyone can join, it is an interactive brainstorming.

Translation:

Don't you dare interrupt my monologue!

English people say:

That is quite a good idea.

Translation:
You are a donkey and you are just embarrassing yourself.

English people say:
I am not sure I like it.

Translation:
To me, it sucks.

English people say:
Not a bad idea.

Translation:
I wish that was my idea. I wonder how I could steal it.

English people say:
Very interesting.

Translation:
I wasn't listening. And to be honest, I don't even know who you are.

English people say:
I will definitely consider it.

Translation:
I will definitely not consider it.

English people say:
Any comments?

Translation:
Please remain silent.

English people say:
I would like to add a few minor comments.

Translation:
Be prepared for a two hours' speech.

English people say:
Not really my main expertise.

Translation:
I don't have a clue what the hell are you talking about.

English people say:
Yes, of course, I will consider your pay rise.

Translation:
Yes, of course, I will consider your pay rise next year or the year after. But most likely I will fire you before then.

English people say:
Are you sure?

Translation:
I am sure you are talking nonsense.

English people say:
It really doesn't matter.

Translation:
If we didn't live in the twenty-first century I would call a duel and you would be dead.

English people say:
I am completely fine, honestly.

Translation:
On the way home I will jump from Tower Bridge.

English people say:
The meeting wasn't too bad.

Translation:
I got fired.

English people say:
I am sorry to hear you are leaving. Good luck with your new job. We will really miss you. A lot.

Translation:

Sorry, what was your name again?

English people say:

You got promoted? Good for you!

Translation:

It is only good for you. It will be hell for the rest of us.

English people say:

Go ahead. I will join you later.

Translation:

The last thing I want is to socialise with you after work. It is already killing me to see your face Monday to Friday, eight hours per day. Where is the nearest exit?

18

HOW TO MAKE THE
ENGLISH FEEL UNEASY

THERE ARE DAYS when you get up on the wrong side of the bed and you feel irritable without any particular reason. On these days you say things you don't really mean and hurt people unintentionally.

On other days you get up on the right side of the bed, but still you hurt people.

That's because you are a human being. And in every human being there is that little devil who occasionally enjoys pissing people off. Of course nobody admits it, but still, that's the truth.

Pissing off someone is so much easier (and way more fun) than pleasing someone.

If you want to piss off a Hungarian the best thing to do is to tell them one of the hungry Hungarian jokes, like:

'Where are you from?'

'Hungary.'

'Me too. I'm starving.'

You can put a fake smile on your face the first time, and remain silent on the hundredth time. But when you reach the thousandth time, with the other person laughing out loud as if they just invented the best joke ever on earth, then either you are Mahatma Gandhi or you will turn violent.

Pissing off Romanians is even easier. Just tell them proudly that you know Romania very well and you think that their capital Budapest is the most beautiful city in the world. They will become extremely furious and I really don't know why. Budapest is such a magnificent city that Romanians should feel honoured that their capital is always mixed up with it.*

If you want to piss off the French, tell them that you prefer Italian cuisine rather than French. If you want to piss off Italians just ask them about the

* The capital of Romania is Bucharest.

Mafia. For the Colombians, ask them how to grow a coca plant. These questions are the best if you ask right after introduction, like:

—*Hi, my name is Angela Kiss.*
—*Hi, I am Ettore Rossi.*
—*Your name sounds Italian.*
—*Yes, I am an Italian.*
—*So, tell me, what is new with the Cosa Nostra nowadays?*

They will be just as pissed off if you ask them about Berlusconi's 'bunga bunga' parties.

There are many ways to piss off The English too. But, believe me, there is something even more satisfying for your little inner devil than pissing them off. Making them a little uneasy is way more fun.

Pissing someone off is explicit, and English people never talk or act explicitly. And if you just make them feel a little uneasy, they will be unsure whether you did it on purpose or just by accident. English people are absolutely not assertive folk, so won't ask straight questions about the deliberateness of your behaviour, so they will just feel frustrated and confused. Which is great fun, believe me.

Let's say there is a queue. If you entered a queue and stood not right behind the last person but before him or her, then that person will be very pissed off. Instead, stand neither before the last person nor behind, but next to him or her. This will result in an extremely uneasy feeling for the poor English person. Actually so uneasy and frustrated that they would rather let you jump their position.

Another example:

Let's say you are in a restaurant with an English person and you send back your food because you are not satisfied with it. You might look rude and, most of all, they would be pissed off since in their eyes any fuss about your ice-cold dinner being decorated with a bunch of chef's hairs is unnecessary and so alien. And you would lose a dinner mate forever. Instead, you should just tell them that you are not entirely satisfied with your dinner and will refuse to pay the service charge. The best time to tell this is in the middle of dinner. They will feel so uneasy that they will lose their appetite, not ask for dessert at all, feel guilty and eventually offer to pay for the both of you.

Another easy way to disturb English people is to make them unsure. You just have to ask one simple question after they make any assertion: 'Are you sure?' Believe me: they will panic so much they would eventually start sweating.

Actually, if you are the kind of person that enjoys making people sweat, then ask English people to introduce themselves or say something about themselves in front of a large audience. (In this case 'large audience' means more than one person, including themselves.)

If you sit on an airplane and you tell the English person sitting next to you that you have a bomb in your bag, they would probably be pissed off. Not as much pissed off as if you were talking to them all the time during the journey, but still, quite pissed off. Instead, don't turn off your mobile when the stewardess asks to do so. This will make The English feel desperately uneasy, fearing that your mobile signal will confuse the navigation system of the airplane resulting in a catastrophic crash on a remote island. Breaking rules is the most powerful way to make English uneasy.

Public displays of emotion are another good way to make English people feel uneasy. And I am not talking about kissing passionately with hands running everywhere. Just holding hands with your girlfriend or boyfriend is enough.

Similarly, The English don't even introduce their partner to others as such, they just say 'she/he is my friend'. The status of their 'friend' changes to 'girl-friend/boyfriend' only when wedding invitations are sent out, never before. So, if your little devil wants to make an English person uneasy when accompanied, all you have to do is to seek a clarification on the exact nature of their relationship status. Ask with your most innocent face, 'You mean your girlfriend/boyfriend, right?' They will both look immediately at their shoes and start a long story with a multiple combinations of the following words: well, right, yes of course, not at all, absolutely, indeed, lovely weather.

Sometimes you don't even need to be with an English person to make him or her feel uneasy. Try calling The English from an unknown number. The best victim you can choose is a work colleague since you can eye witness their panic and listen to all the conspiracy theories about who was calling them. Warning: Don't call them more than three times a day because that could make them change their number (rather than take the phone call and see who called them).

I have just realised that listing all that makes English people feel uneasy would result in a chapter as long as the whole British encyclopaedia, with the extra volumes of yearly updates. Probably I should focus on 'How not to make The English feel uneasy'. But, to be honest, I cannot think of anything. Which will probably make my English readers uneasy.

19

HOW TO COMMUTE

Fʀᴏᴍ ᴍᴏɴᴅᴀʏ ᴛᴏ Friday, with my hour-long journey to work, I can proudly consider myself very much part of the 'happy' community of average English commuters. But on Saturdays and Sundays when I 'play writer' (as my friends says) my commuting time reduces to zero: I just wake up, open my eyes, turn on my laptop and as if by magic I am ready at my workplace (my bed) in my work uniform (nightdress). From that position commuting seems a complete waste of time.

The only advantage of commuting is that there is always something (something typical I mean) happening during the journey to talk about (more precisely: complain about) during working hours.

English people love complaining. A lot. And not only about big tragedies like someone happening to commit suicide jumping in front of their train (the real tragedy being the delay, since suicide in England belongs to the 'mind your own business' category) but also about small things. When I say small things I mean small things for us aliens, not for The English in whose eyes they can easily be huge affairs. Let's say it is summer and you are on an overcrowded bus with the air conditioning broken, therefore it is boiling hot. English people would never do such a complicated social thing as asking the closest person to the window to open it. They would rather roast to death and then complain about it for the rest of the day. It's the same thing when, let's say, someone puts his or her bag on a free seat. Asking somebody to remove his or her bag is such a big deal for The English. They prefer to stand still staring and cursing that person secretly, just so they can complain about their rudeness for a week.

One of the activities that most annoys English commuters on public transport is eating. When I first arrived in England I took the early airplane from Budapest to Stansted and then the 8.15 a.m. Stansted Express to the city. By the time I was halfway on the train I started to be really hungry. (Yes, a hungry Hungarian. Ha-ha!) Luckily enough I had a seat with a table, so I opened the foil wrapper of my 100 per cent genuine Hungarian home-made sandwich, made by my mum, and I started my little breakfast picnic. I still remember how nicely my Hungarian smoked sausage paprika sandwich with mustard smelled. At the time, I thought that the English people looking at me secretly from behind their newspapers and laptops were craving my mouth-watering gourmet treat. But I was very wrong. It was not Mum's paprika delicacy but my uncivilised alien behaviour. And I can clearly see now how those English commuters poisoned their colleagues and families for the following three or four days com-plaining about that paprika girl on the train.

Please note: Thou Shalt Not, under any circum-stances, eat on a train, tube or bus, not even if you are the only passenger on the upper decker of a double-decker and you are about to starve to death. Thou Shalt behave on public transport as a human being. A human English being. And human

English beings never pollute public transport with that un-typical alien smoked nuisance. The only accepted civilised behaviour is to play the invisible person: hide behind a newspaper or book or play with your mobile or look at your shoes. Strictly your shoes, no others shoes, as you always must mind your own business.

Apart from finding things to complain about, it is interesting to notice how English people refuse the fact of commuting. They interpret their journey not as spending time on public transport between their home and their workplaces but they pretend to be *still* at home (for example, in their bathroom putting on their make-up) or *already* at their workplace (talking about confidential business issues). The most extraordinary activity I've seen on public transport (apart from the Saturday night drunk pole dancers on the tube carriage pole) was someone peeling a potato on the way home. But they wouldn't eat a cooked potato. It seems like *public* transport is the only place where English people don't mind acting *private*. If in England there was any public display of affection (which there is not), then be sure it would happen most on an overcrowded tube carriage just next to you.

Once, for a short while, I had the pleasure to commute from Sutton to north London. According to Transport for London, Sutton is in Zone 5, however it felt more like I was from Zone 55. From door to door it was a one-and-a-half-hour journey, totalling three hours travelling time per day. That commute completely changed my personality. Before, my motto was 'make love not war' and my role models were Gandhi and Mandela. But after a week of commuting I came to the conclusion that I must be the lineal descendent of our great warrior, Attila the Hun (or as other nations called him: The God's Fury), and I realised that sometimes battle is a must. Public Transport Battle.

Of course, The English are serene and polite folk, so these wars are more like the Cold War: they seem to be not much more than a mere political tension, but everyone knows that any time it could end up with blood being shed. It is obvious that, with my 44 kilograms, I am not going to get my way with any physical warfare escalation, so my first warrior strategy was based on simple but lethal weapons: the miniskirt and high heels. And guess what, it worked! But only on men and only on the very first week. On the second week, when all Public

Transport Warriors standing every morning at the same platform realised that my journeys the week before weren't just single trips, they started considering me as a fellow commuter, which translates as another being to obstruct them and slow them down, to fight for the limited seats and the limited standing places and an additional consumer of the already limited amount of breathable air in the carriages. Then I realised that, when it comes to Public Transport Wars, aliens can only win individual fights. Public Transport Wars are just like all other tough wars where there is no place for friendship, no time for a smile and not even a moment for 'Good morning'.

Spotting Great English Public Transport Warriors is easy. They know exactly where to stand on the platform so that the bus, train or tube doors will stop and open just right by them. Also, they know where to get on the train/tube so they will be right by the exit when they get off. Always in a hurry, they walk fast, talk fast, check the watches or smartphones fast, and they never, I mean never, enjoy some smoked sausage sandwich during the peak hour. And, believe me, you don't want to mess with these Great English

Public Transport Warriors, because they are not the typical, polite, fair-player English, they are the typical city workers, which is a complete different species. They are on a win-or-die mission.

And what do these people win?

No less than a longer life!

You don't believe me, do you?

Let me do some maths for you. When Great English Public Transport Warriors open their mouth (or just raise their eyebrows) the crowd opens in front them and people immediately give them what they want: free way. (If you want a free way too, my advice is to play the first lady game: let them fight and do the dirty job, like presidents do, and you just follow them so very closely, and smile and enjoy all the benefit of their victory.) For them, the gained free way can easily result in catching an earlier tube. Yes, I know, there are tubes in every two or three minutes, but catching an earlier tube could mean to catch an earlier connection and that, in total, according to my daily statistics, can result in 9 minutes saved per day, which is 45 minutes per week, which is 39 hours or 1.625 days per year.

Not bad, isn't it?

And what do all Great English Public Transport Warriors do with this 1.625 extra days per year?

They spend it with their favourite (typical) activity, of course: complain about Public Transport.

21

HOW TO DINE

GEORGE MIKES SAID 'On the Continent people have good food; in England people have good table manners.'

Today, the newspapers and television are full of talk about food, but actually nothing changed since 1946.

22

HOW TO UNDERSTAND UNDERSTATEMENT AND UNDERACHIEVEMENT

GEORGE MIKES WROTE about understatement: 'It is not just a speciality of the English sense of humour; it is a way of life.'

For us aliens, understanding English understatement and its purpose can be as hard as it is for English people to understand why aliens kiss and hug when they greet each other.

Understatement in humour is somehow more understandable (although aliens don't see it as amusing as The English), but when it comes to everyday life its use remains a mystery to aliens.

Aliens use understatement very rarely and only if it is reasonable, but English people use it all the time regardless of its necessity. More confusing, English people use understatement in situations aliens never would.

Understatement is so alien in alien countries that in most languages there is not even a word that exists as a translation for 'understatement'. For example, in most countries there is no translation for the Hungarian word *hálapénz*, which is corrupt gratuity money, hidden in an envelope you give secretly to your doctor after your treatment. It is not compulsory, of course, but very advisable if you want to stay alive. Compared to this, England's NHS doesn't sound that bad, right? Since the method of bribing doctors for better treatment doesn't exist in England, there was never a need for a word that describes it. Another example, the Hungarian word *káröröm* is also non-existent in English; it means: pleasure obtained from the misfortunes of others. English people absolutely disapprove of such ruthless behaviour; therefore they don't even have a word for it. (The Germans have: *Schadenfreude*.) There is no equivalent English word for the Italian word *afa*, which means suffocating heat, because in

England such suffocating heat (or any other heat) does not exist. The English word 'understatement' in alien countries is the same – they don't practise understatement, so there was never a need for the word. That is why I decided to help aliens understand understatement.

According to Oxford dictionary, understatement is 'the presentation of something as being smaller or less good or important than it really is'. According to Collins dictionary understatement is 'the act or an instance of stating something in restrained terms, or as less than it is'.

I know exactly what is arising in your alien mind now: Why would they do that? Why would they soften bad news or criticism or demands?

First of all, English people don't like emotional emphasis. Pragmatism never goes along with drama, and understatement is a pragmatic approach indeed. Second, English people have fears of causing offence. They are too polite to hurt others explicitly. They always want to make other people feel better, to make the gloomy truth or reality easier to deal with.

Let's be honest, sometimes, we aliens do the same with children and with people emotionally not fully developed.

I am not saying that English people are emotionally undeveloped, but there is some truth in George Mikes saying: 'The British are brave people. They can face anything, except reality.'

And understatement is the best weapon against reality.

As an example always explains things better than the theory, let me try this:

One of the most famous understatements was made by Eric Moody in 1982. For aliens, he might sound like a humourist but he was the British Airways pilot who, after flying through a cloud of volcanic ash which caused all four engines to fail, made this announcement to the passengers:

'Ladies and gentlemen, this is your captain speaking. We have a small problem. All four engines have stopped. We are doing our damnedest to get them going again. I trust you are not in too much distress.'

I am sure that for alien passengers it sounded like a cruel joke, but for English passengers it was a usual and reassuring way of communication.

Just like understatement, you can also observe self-deprecation about achievements, self-mockery and boasting about underachievement on national level too. The latter can create a lot of confusion in aliens' minds, especially aliens like me from a former socialist country. In ex-communist states, reaching The Plan was never enough. Overachievement was the only achievement. I believe that our grandparents' Stakhanovism is still in our blood. We think that working hard and knowing everything is just a 'must-do' and we are under secret and constant monitoring. Therefore, if there is something we cannot do or don't know about, we feel embarrassment and humiliation, and so we try to hide it or pretend to know.

I remember when one of my English colleagues mentioned his favourite writer, someone I had never heard of before. The fact that two other English colleagues didn't recognise his name either was not a relief for me. But what was the difference between us? I felt the urge to know everything about that writer (and of course I did as soon as I had a chance to look): his writing achievements, his books with their plot and publishing dates, the author's birthdate and birthplace and everything about his and his family's life and the life of all the other people who were ever in contact with him. I checked all the information in three different languages, so as to not miss anything important. What about my two English colleagues? They simply admitted they never ever heard his name, and proudly recalled other similar 'funny' situations when someone mentioned something famous and they didn't know about it either.

It was shocking.

Not the fact that they didn't know that writer, of course, but the fact that they laughed about their ignorance. And before you think that it was an example of English honesty I must disappoint you. It wasn't. It was a typical example of playing up their underachievement. Why? Because English people's self-confidence is so high that they can afford to admit negative information about themselves. Even more, they can boast and mock themselves about it. Of course, they prefer to mock anybody else, but themselves can be fine too.

23

HOW TO HAVE A HOLIDAY

Eⁿglish people love being on holiday. They like all sorts of holidays: short and long holidays, five-star and starless holidays, holidays in England and abroad too.

The shorter holidays in England always have unexpected surprises. You have a certain plan, but transport companies have other plans. They close tube and rail lines and roads and your whole journey changes. Thanks to tube and rail replacement buses and road closures you can easily end up in another part of the city or country than you intended and you can effortlessly spend most of a day being lost there. Such small trips give huge pleasure to The English. Not because they like to explore unfamiliar places but because they enjoy complaining.

Seaside weekend holidays in England are also good resources for complaining. If it rains, English people sit and complain about the bad weather in their sea-view hotel rooms, if it is sunny they sit and complain in their car about the hot weather and the traffic jam they are stuck in, since if it is over 15 degrees all English people immediately head to the sea.

When it comes to holidays, English people's preferences resemble very much their class system. Upper-class and working-class people are proud of their status, upper-middle class is still acceptable, but lower-middle class is a complete embarrassment.* This is reflected in the English person's holiday accommodation preferences. English people proudly admit spending time in expensive five-star luxury hotels or in starless bed & breakfast for a fair price. (Don't think that posh hotels are full of upper-class people and B&Bs with lower-class people, quite the opposite.) A four-star hotel is still kind of

* Most of England's population belongs to the lower-middle class.

acceptable. But having a holiday in a one- or two- or three-star hotel is a total embarrassment, sleeping rough under a bridge would still be a better choice. Similarly, if English people rent a car during their holiday they would go either for a luxury car or for a Skoda. Choosing a Fiat Punto or a Volkswagen Golf is very un-English, they would rather travel on a gypsy horse caravan. It's the same rule for food: at least five star but preferably a Michelin-starred restaurant or eating fish and chips out of newspaper in a dodgy street market. No middle way. Middle-classness is very un-English.

Extremity can be observed in English people's holidays abroad too. Some English people visit other countries to discover different cultures and architecture, and to meet different nations and try different food, however, most of them prefer Englishness even during their holiday in a foreign country: they fly with British Airways, they stay in holiday resorts mostly with English holidaymakers, they eat English breakfast or porridge and drink English tea with milk served by an English-speaking staff, and they socialise only with English people, possibly on a grass tennis court or golf course. These are The English that visit the same holiday resort every single year. They know all the staff's names and have photos with all of them; they know which room has the best view, which bartender does the best cocktail and what is the tastiest meal on the menu, and they always ask for the same room, the same drink and same food. Being adventurous on holiday is very un-English and only rarely you can observe an English person breaking this routine.

Surprisingly, English people like each other abroad more than in England. For example, if two English people sit on the bus next to each other in England, they play the invisible game during the whole journey. The only acceptable conversation is to ask for directions. (FYI: English people prefer to be lost for days or even for weeks than looking inexpert and ask for directions. This, by the way, is the other typical way for English people to have short holidays in England.) Now, if the same two English people meet abroad, they greet each other enthusiastically, a friendship sparks immediately and they share all sorts of personal information and emotions that they would never do even with their best friend in England. (Only with their pets.)

English people always wait for their holiday flights at one of England's airports without the tiniest trace of happiness or enthusiasm. They push their airport trolley with complete apathy and stand in the queue without looking or talking to each other. But as soon as their airplane leaves England, slowly but surely they change and become extroverts (not fully extrovert, only borderline extrovert) and their stiff upper lips soften to a sort of smile and they eventually become talkative.

Some very brave adrenalin junkie English people change a lot when abroad and become very wild, and they take pride in sharing all their adventures in every possible social media channel: drinking tea without milk, going to the beach using sun cream SPF45 instead of SPF50+, using their hairdryer in the bathroom and mingling with local aliens.

Typical English holidaymakers prefer not to mingle with foreigners since they strongly believe that they already have too many of them in England. The last thing they need during their holiday is to see and meet more aliens. Actually, that is the main reason why they choose a holiday abroad, to escape from aliens who occupy England.

You must always keep in mind the most important alien rule George Mikes observed: roles never change. English people never consider themselves as foreigners, not even when abroad. For example, if they visit Hungary, they are not aliens in Hungary. Hungarians are the aliens. Yes, Hungarians are aliens in their own country. Location doesn't change rules.

According to The English, there are too many foreigners in foreign countries. But they still prefer them there than in England, therefore they don't complain about it too much and too loud. But they complain about everything else: the weather is too hot in the beach resort and too cold in the ski resort (although before their booking they always check the last five years of weather forecasts for their holiday destination), the white sandy beach is too white (therefore it hurts their eyes) and too sandy (therefore they always have to clean their swimming costume from sand), the sea is too wet and too wavy or not wavy enough or there are too many or not enough fish in the sea (although they only put their toe into the sea, they prefer the swimming pool, which of course is never good enough, as it would be in England), in fully equipped apartments abroad there are no teaspoons, only coffee spoons, there is not a single bloody shop in the Himalayas that sells Jaffa Cakes, and they constantly complain

They look at their camera and they surprisingly realise that they smile in the photos and seem happy.

about local aliens who don't speak English (although they don't speak any alien languages on their own, the only alien words they know is '*una cerveza por favor*' and '*dos cerveza por favor*' and '*Voulez-vous coucher avec moi?*').

On the way back to England, English people's suitcases are full of local handicraft souvenirs (and alcohol and cigars) and their camera full of photos. When their plane leaves they look back once more to the alien country from the airplane window and they think that after all it wasn't a too bad holiday.

They look at their camera and they surprisingly realise that they smile in the photos and seem happy. Maybe they were happy indeed. But happy is easy. Every alien can do that. Being typical, being English. That is unique.

And then secretly, and strictly only if nobody sees them, they allow a last smile before arriving to England and clenching their jaw once again.

24

HOW TO BE EQUAL

'A LL ANIMALS ARE equal, but some animals are more equal than others' was written by George Orwell.

Our Hungarian George said '… the English remain staunch believers in equality. Equality is a notion the English have given to humanity. Equality means that you are just as good as the next man but the next man is not half as good as you are.'

In present-day England, everybody is considered to be equal. But all English people look down upon all aliens (which of course also include the Welsh, Scottish and Irish).

All English people look down upon all English people with alien ancestors.

All aliens look down upon all other aliens who arrived in England later than them. And all of them look down upon aliens who still live in their homeland.

All Western European aliens living in England look down upon all Eastern European aliens living in England.

All Eastern European aliens living in England look down upon all other aliens who are from further east or south.

All aliens from EU countries look down upon aliens from non-EU countries, especially illegal immigrants.

Everybody looks down upon people from Birmingham.

Brummies look down on everybody else.

All Londoners look down upon everybody who doesn't live in London, especially those who don't live in London but commute to London every day.

All English people who live by the seaside or in the countryside look down upon city dwellers.

All London City workers look down upon everybody who doesn't work in the City of London.

All west Londoners look down upon east Londoners.

All people who studied at Cambridge look down upon people who studied at Oxford.

All people who studied at Oxford look down upon people who studied at Cambridge.

All people who were sent overseas to study at Harvard look down upon both Oxford and Cambridge alumni.

All people who live on benefits in England look down upon people who work for their living.

All people who shop at M&S look down upon people who shop at Sainsbury's, who look down upon people shopping at Morrisons or Asda. All of them look down upon people who only shop at Lidl or Aldi.

All people who fly from/to Heathrow Terminal 5 look down upon people who fly from/to any other England's airport.

All the *Guardian* and the *Independent* readers look down upon people who read the *Sun*. All of them look down upon *Metro* newspaper readers. And all of them look down upon old-fashioned people who read books.

Everybody looks down upon people who like *The X Factor* or *EastEnders*. All of them look down upon people who don't have television.

From this you can easily see that the only respected member of the English society is the Queen.

(Although she has alien ancestors.)

25

HOW TO FAKE
MODERN ENGLISH

Dear fellow aliens,

Have you ever heard the famous quotation 'It is not the strongest of the species that survives, nor the most intelligent that survives. It is the one that is most adaptable to change.'

Some people believe it was said by Charles Darwin, but I am not here to discuss that, I am here to observe how this applies to the aliens living in England: It is not the strongest of the aliens that survives in England, nor the most intelligent that survives. It is the one that is most adaptable to change.

Obviously you cannot change and become English but here is my 50 best tips on how to fake it:

1. Don't admit that you speak foreign languages. Moreover, work very hard on forgetting them, especially your mother tongue.
2. Don't talk clearly. Always mutter and mumble.
3. While talking, refrain yourself from non-verbal communication. Poker face. Poker body.
4. Don't use adjectives. The only exception: nice.
5. Never speak with perfect grammar. If you speak English too well, it is a clear sign that you are an alien.
6. Get rid of your bad alien habit of looking at English people's lips in the hope to understand their accent easier. They will think that you want to kiss them.
7. Don't ask 'excuse me?' or 'pardon?', only aliens do that (and lower-class English people, but they are only slightly better than aliens). Instead, ask, 'What?'
8. Don't greet people if you enter somewhere. They will think that you are eccentric and looking for extra attention.
9. Talk about '5-A-Day' and 'two-day diet' healthy

eating all the time, but eat a whole packet of vinegar crisp twice a day.

10. Declare your favourite English recipes are baked beans on toast and chicken tikka masala.

11. Brown sauce is your new ketchup.

12. Drink the average English quantity of tea: 3.32 cups per day.

13. Always talk about the greatness of 'Made in England' products, however, in a pub order a Czech beer or a Jamaican spirit, in a restaurant order French food, wear Italian clothes and shoes and only see American movies.

14. Always talk about the greatness of London but move to the countryside as soon as you can.

15. Your DIY project doesn't mean anymore cutting down a tree in the forest and gathering reed for your roof. It means going to Homebase, buying a hammer and a nail and hanging up a picture. (And hurting yourself badly, rushing to the emergency for the usual NHS paracetamol and codeine, and the next day in your workplace boasting about your wound like a proud war hero.)

16. If you mention your garden you can forget understatement, for once, and only talk in superlatives

like it is a size of the Hyde Park. It doesn't matter if it is only 10mm and it is all concrete.

17. You shall not know the conversion systems. If someone mentions kilometres instead of miles, litres instead of pints, kilograms instead of stone and Celsius instead of Fahrenheit, you must look at that person as if she or he is insane.

18. If you are a man and you have a shed you must talk about it like a king about his kingdom. Your shed is the only place where you find peace and harmony. (Apart from your local pub.)

19. If you enter someone's house don't take off your shoes, especially if the carpet is white. If you take off your shoes English people will look at you just as shocked as the Japanese if you don't take off your shoes before stepping on the tatami.

20. If you say something about foreigners always add the word 'but'. For example: 'I like foreigners, but …'

21. Never give a tip if you order a drink. And most of the time not even after a meal.

22. Never be ashamed of asking for tap water in restaurants. It is only embarrassing and a sign of poorness in Europe. (According to The

English, England is not part of Europe. Never has been, never will be. England is England, not part of anything.)

23. Whenever you ask something from a waiter or waitress you always must apologise for disturbing him or her.

24. Sharing food is just as un-English as sharing feelings.

25. Your morning hobby is to confuse alien baristas. Be eccentric; never ask for anything simpler than an iced-cinnamon-mocha-chocolate-Frappuccino.

26. Hunter boots and a Barbour coat are a must. Burberry is a not a bad choice either.

27. If you are an office worker, wear your business suit with trainers and a rucksack.

28. Be reserved and live isolated. But don't close your curtains, let every passer-by see your life like you are a fish in an aquarium.

29. Don't hug people. Only if they are the warmest object near you and you are about to freeze to death.

30. Be always unsure. Especially during sex. Keep asking 'are you okay?' and 'is everything all right?' like you are not sure what you are doing.

After sex don't reach for your cigar. Reach for your cup of tea.

31. After sex don't reach for your cigar. Reach for your cup of tea.

32. If it is about Christmas cards, quantity wins against quality. The more you send with the least emotional wish the more English you appear. My advice: 'Merry Xmas.' with a dot, not with an exclamation mark. Exclamation marks mean emotions, therefore you'd be uncovered as the alien you are.

33. Always do your Christmas shopping in the last week and on Oxford Street. And always make a New Year's resolution that you will never do it again. And forget this before January is over.

34. Don't break rules. Ever.

35. The only rule you are allowed to break is cross-ing the road without pressing the button and then waiting for the green signal. Breaking that traffic rule is still more English than making such a big fuss as pressing the button to stop the traffic and having all the cars' pas-sengers looking at you while you walk on the crossing. Only aliens do such eccentric per-formances. (Risking your life is still a better choice.)

36. When you drive a car and arrive at a round-about, always panic about who goes first. Rather wait for a whole day and let every single car go before you than make an impolite decision.

37. Never talk about money or income.

38. Say 'sorry' not only to human beings and animals but to objects too. Like doors and tables (if you bump into them) or cash machines (if you press a wrong button).

39. Get drunk every Friday after work. Best to start at lunchtime. Preferably Thursday lunchtime.

40. Never take a selfie with a red phone box, postbox or double-decker.

41. Enter Harrods as if it is a shop. Only aliens behave as if it is a museum.

42. Littering is a must. Not because you are rude or dirty but because you are thoughtful and you are helping poor aliens to have jobs.

43. Sleep in the recovery position. Just in case.

44. Mind the gap.

45. Stand behind the yellow line.

46. No standing on the upper deck or stairs.

47. Don't use any electrical devices in the bathroom.

48. No sex in the kitchen or bathroom or shed.

49. Never talk to strangers.

50. Especially, don't talk to strangers who are aliens.

26

HOW TO BE A DINNER
GUEST IN ENGLAND

I WOULD NEVER HAVE expected that one day I, an alien, would be invited to an English home for dinner, so it was with a big excitement that I accepted.

Later, when I remembered my waitress days, all my excitement vanished completely.

During my waitress era, my favourite work activity was to watch customers. (I hope this confession will not give English people a new phobia.) Alien customers always came to enjoy the food and the drink, to have a great night out and to socialise. What about English customers? To be honest, I really don't know. Of course they ate all the food and drank all the drinks I put in front of them, without a single word, but I never had the feeling that they really, I mean truly from the bottom of their stomach, enjoyed it. My best guess is because English people focus not on the taste of the meal but on their table manners: how to behave properly, how to sit properly, how to order properly, how to cut the meat properly without hurting themselves or others (health and safety above all) and how to manage their acrobatic performance to put every single pea on the wrong side of their fork.

I understand that English food has never had a reputation to be proud of, that is why they focus on table manners instead, but I believe it is now time to change. It is time to learn how to enjoy eating. Eating should be a pleasure! England is full of amazing restaurants. I am not talking about English restaurants, of course, but about alien restaurants. Have you ever seen a restaurant in England with an advertisement on it 'English restaurant'? I have only seen 'Turkish restaurant', 'Greek restaurant', 'Italian restaurant', 'French restaurant', 'Spanish Tapas restaurant',

'Thai restaurant', 'Argentinian restaurant' and all the other European and Asian and African and South American restaurants, but I have never seen an advertisement like 'English restaurant'; only 'English pub'. And that explains everything. My advice to The English is to go to any alien restaurant and observe how aliens enjoy their meal. Think of yourself as an open-minded zoologist who examines chimpanzees in the hope you might learn something from them.

My other waitress observation was that English people doesn't like sharing. Not just the meal itself, but also sharing the pleasure of eating together. Our alien customers always seemed enjoying the socialising part of the dinner a little more than the meal itself. English people always seemed to enjoy reading a newspaper or watching their watch constantly or socialising with others online rather than focusing on their offline companions sitting opposite them. Believe me; not having a strong internet signal in a restaurant upsets modern English people more than not having a Sunday roast on the Sunday menu.

Now you might understand why I was scared to have dinner at The English. Also, I was alarmed, as I'd heard that for English people the expression 'cooking something' normally means 'reheating a ready-made meal in the microwave' or, in some extreme cases, 'adding a Worcester sauce to a take-away food'.

But I was also curious.

My dad always said that, even if you don't have weapons, never go to warzones without a shield, so before leaving the house I checked couple of Jane Austen movies about how to behave properly. I also watched the last episodes of *EastEnders* and *The X Factor*, and read the most relevant BBC news and glossy magazine gossips, so I'd have a clue about the hottest topics, because English people like to talk about neutral and meaningless subjects.

My colleague, Caroline, said to arrive about 6 p.m., so I arrived at 6.22. By that time her husband's colleagues were already there, a Swiss and a German engineer (I am sure they arrived exactly at 1800 hours), and they were talking about the mechanics of World War II tanks, so I headed to the kitchen to see Caroline. She was a new colleague of mine, and they had just moved to London from Wickhambreaux. In the first weeks I was absolutely sure she was an alien because she was so friendly, she always greeted everyone with a lovely smile, she listened to people with honest interest and she seemed enjoying the foreign colleagues' company more than The English. I was surprised to find out that she was aboriginal English. It seemed that countryside English people are less typical English and more borderline alien.

But in her kitchen she was typical English: if something is not going according to plan, English people panic immediately. Three cookery books were open on the table and Jamie Oliver was on YouTube. There was some suspicious yellow something in a pot on the hob, sticky rice in a saucepan, and one English girl checking M&S's closing time, one French girl sending constant text messages (I guess: 'S.O.S. save me from this *merde*!') and Caroline panicking and apologising for not cooking an English pie but now that they moved to London she wanted to look more cosmopolitan and that is why she decided to cook Asian food. As you see, moving to a multicultural city and become cosmopolitan is very hard.

The situation was saved by an Italian man who, despite being an engineer, was still more interested in food than in wars or vehicle mechanics. His entrance to the kitchen was a great opportunity for the French girl to escape. She disappeared so mysteriously that even the world-famous Hungarian illusionist Harry Houdini would be envious. The other English woman suggested she could drive to M&S to pick up some ready-made food (I think her intention was to escape and never come back) or to order a home-delivery pizza. The Italian man said if any of that happens he would rather leave. (As you see Italians are the opposite of The English: they talk explicitly without hesitation.) Caroline panicked even more. Mr Italy opened the pot's lid (and didn't hide his disgust) and said that: panicking is not part of the Italian lifestyle, freestyle problem solving is their expertise, we shall trust him.

By the time he finished cooking that Asian dinner with a life-saving Italian touch, two more English couples had arrived and they opened a bottle of champagne to congratulate Mr Italy on saving the dinner (typical English: they were more interested in alcohol than in food). (Mr Dinner Saver refused to celebrate with French champagne, so we opened a bottle of Prosecco too. Italian patriotism is unbelievable!)

After all the food was eaten, everyone focused on alcohol. English people and alcohol are never a good combination so I decided to leave. Mr Italiano offered to drive me home.

In his car (no, it wasn't a Vespa) he said that he was looking at me during the meal (as you see not only Hungarian waitresses enjoy looking at people when they eat) and he saw that I hardly ate anything, he believes I must be hungry. I nodded and smiled. I smiled because he didn't mention any hungry Hungarian jokes.

He said he is hungry too (for the same reason I was: despite his life-saving touch, the dinner didn't reached either Hungarian or Italian standards), so he stopped the car at the first shop.

After I picked up a sandwich I found him in the pasta section. (Italians are very predictable.) He spent 4 minutes and 39 seconds there, he checked all the labels of all the pastas, and then he finally chose one.

'What are you doing with that triangle sandwich?' he looked at my dinner disgustedly. 'Put it back. I am going to cook some pasta for you.'

Normally I would never accept such late-night dinner invitation to a stranger's house but after eye witnessing his performance of breaking the Guinness Record of Pasta Shopping he was clearly more interested in pastas than in me.

In all, it was a very instructive night for me. First, I learnt that never underestimate an Italian man if it is about pasta. Or about women. Second, always think twice before accepting an English dinner invitation.

A month later Caroline invited me for lunch. And this time I indeed thought twice before accepting it. My first thought was that it is on Sunday, and English people's stomach doesn't accept any other food on Sunday than Sunday roast (which is their traditional food therefore they must be masters of cooking it), and my second thought was that, after all, I am a typical alien who enjoys the socialising part of a dining more than the meal itself and Caroline and her friends are such warm and funny people that it is my pleasure to dine with them (even if the food goes wrong).

I didn't regret my decision. That roast chicken was the best Sunday roast I have ever eaten in my life (including in restaurants), and her banoffee pie was so delicious that even Mr Italiano asked for its recipe. The French girl remained silent. French people will never admit that anyone could be better in the kitchen than them.

27

HOW TO DATE

Dating on the Continent means a romantic rendezvous with the purpose of two people getting to know each other and explore whether there is a hint of spark, a possibility for a romantic relationship and then a happily ever after until they die.

Dating in England is different.

First of all because English people don't like at all other people knowing them, and second, because English people are romantically impaired.

Dates should have no rules to be followed; they should be spontaneous and adaptable to circumstances, based on the mood and interest, the weather, the feeling, what's going on in the moment. But being spontaneous is very un-English. English people prefer to follow rules and traditions and rites. Therefore the traditional part of dating works very well for The English: Englishman suggests a place, Englishman books a table, they consume the ordered drink or meal, and the Englishman pays the bill or they go Dutch.

'What is the problem?' aliens might ask.

Well, there are three enormously huge question marks about the above English date.

1. Where and how two people meet before the first date?
2. What do they talk about on the first date?
3. What happens to English people after their first date has concluded?

1. On where and how two English people meet before the first date

Since English people hardly ask a stranger even for directions, asking out someone met on the street, café, library or bus, etc., never happens.

Sometimes you see English people going out

to pub, bar or disco with friends, standing awkwardly together drinking beer or gin and tonic and waiting for something 'romantic' to happen. Usually nothing happens apart from everybody getting drunk, which is hardly romantic. So, typically, instead of meeting Mr or Miss Right they meet Mr or Miss Right Now, which lasts as long as there is enough alcohol circulating in the blood vessel. Being drunk is the only situation when English people completely avoid health and safety rules. Apart from that they always like to play safe, even in dating. That is why most of the time they go on a date with someone they already know a bit, like friends of friends or work colleagues or other acquaintances. Taking risks is very un-English.

There is an exception: although speed-dating has a certain level of risk, it is very popular amongst English people. In little villages, for example where I come from, there is no point of going to a speed-date event because you have already known all the existing seven potential dating partners since birth, but in a metropolis like London it is different. Especially for those who enjoy 'pig in a poke' games. In the naive moment when you sign up for speed-dating you tend to dream about meeting Mr

Darcy or David Gandy (Kate Middleton or Katie Price) but the reality is completely different. If you want to know what kind of people you could meet in a speed-dating event, close your book right now and have a look around, walk down the street if you have to: the first 20 people you see easily represent the typical speed-dating population. I am sure this little exercise will make you think twice before signing up for such blind-date events. So why do English people enjoy speed-dating so much? Because on speed-dating people have only two minutes to get to know each other and these two minutes are the perfect amount of time for the small talk that English people are masters of.

Living in the era of social media and dating apps, online dating is also a very popular dating method in England. It perfectly suits the English person's superpower: being the invisible man or woman. They also like to keep their distance, and the internet is perfect for that. Also complimenting someone is easier online than offline; you don't even have to say anything, you just press a 'like' or a 'wink' button and that's it; perfectly suitable for romantically retarded people. For romantic people (aliens) this feels like the death of real love and courtship. It is about quantity rather than a quality, where everyone tries to sell themselves not as human beings but as a disposable goods in sale season. But still, online dating websites are very popular in England and therefore are full of second-hand lovers, most of whom are still in good working condition.

There is only one problem with online dating: sooner or later they must become offline.

If this happens to you, I mean if you finally get an invitation from your English online partner (usually after two or three years), then my advice is never ever ask back explicitly, 'Is it a DATE then?'

2. On what English people talk about on the first date

As an opening, you can expect a substantial amount of complaints about the weather and traffic, and this is pretty much where any enthusiasm finishes. Then an awkward silence comes, because the purpose of dating – i.e. getting to know each other – is very un-English. English people feel extremely uncomfortable talking about themselves, and equally uncomfortable asking personal information of others.

Finding out at your wedding that your partner has a twin brother or sister is not unusual in England.

To avoid all these tortures English people take refuge either in alcohol or the English humour. The combination guarantees a funny night, but after the first date (and the second and the third) you will still have zero information about your date. (Finding out at your wedding that your partner has a twin brother or sister is not unusual in England.) Alcohol is a good thing to comfort themselves with, in case the date goes wrong. And it's the same for the English humour: they can always console themselves that the other person has no sense of humour.

Taking yourself and the dates seriously means coming out and be explicit about your personality and feelings, but it is very un-English. Just as with serious moments, romantic moments are also not part of an English date. With an alien, on the first date you can expect some sweet and charming compliment (in some very extreme cases you can even get a newly invented risotto recipe named after you, with the invitation to a gondola ride the following weekend), but normally on the second date some flowers, on the third date a poem about you or an original love song accompanied by a guitar serenade written just for you. With an English admirer, all you can expect are a couple of pats on your shoulder with the most romantic English compliment: 'Well, after all, it wasn't a bad date, was it?'

3. On what happens to English people after their first date has concluded

Rejecting someone or being rejected is an adult way of communication and therefore it utterly terrifies The English. Even though they are petrified by commitment, they would rather torture themselves with a second and even a third date than talk explicitly. And this is pretty much how most English people end up married.

Now, you understand why dating is un-English, because in England the word 'date' is a synonym of 'marriage'.

28

HOW TO WRITE A LOVE LETTER TO ENGLAND

Although the english are strange creatures I like them a lot and I have lived in England for ten years now. Hungarians and other aliens often ask me, what is it you like so much about England?

I do like rain, for example. I like the black man with the baritone voice working on platform 7 at Highbury & Islington station greeting joyfully arriving passengers on his loudspeaker, making us smiling every single morning. I like the magnificent parks and gardens all over the country open to anyone's enjoyment. I like eating a falafel wrap at Brick Lane market on Sundays. I like Oxfam bookshops. I love all my ex and present bosses and colleagues, who always made me feel at their same level with deep respect and fairness. I love walking along the Regent's Canal. I like queuing in England, because if I am reading a book in the meanwhile nobody takes advantage of me being in my reading bubble by taking over my position. I like the Art Space Gallery. I like that in public places there are disabled toilets and on sanitary bins there is Braille. I like the umbrella-covered street at Borough Market. I am not a big fan of the English cuisine but I must confess I love English desserts a lot, even more than French desserts (*excusez-moi mesdames et messieurs*). I like the Bangladeshi family who works at the greengrocer stall opposite The White Hart Brew Pub at Whitechapel. I like the wooden ducks at Sutton High Street. I like the beautiful inspirational phrase 'Every cloud has a silver lining' (even though meteorologically it is not typical in England). I like the Regent Street Christmas lights. I like The English charity giving. I like that if you get a penalty charge notice or a parking ticket instead of being automatically fined you have a chance to tell your version of the story. I like the Angel Wings at Angel.

You may say that there is rain in Poland too, that Venice is full of amazing canals too, that stunning green landscapes are everywhere in Austria too, that the best falafels are made in the Middle East, and you are certainly right.

But there is one thing that doesn't exist anywhere else in the world: the England's spirit. (When I say spirit, I am not talking about alcohol.) You can catch England's spirit every day if you are an exceptional observer, but there has been recently a big event that displayed this very unique spirit to the whole world. And I am lucky enough to have been part of it too. Indeed, I was one of the Pandemonium Drummers at the London Olympics Opening Ceremony. And not just that. By some miracle my face was chosen to be placed in the middle of the Volunteer Dress worn by all the young women carrying a sign with the country's name and leading the Olympians at the Parade of Nations, which dress is now displayed at the Museum of London.

When I applied I didn't know what to expect, I just wanted to dedicate my time, my effort, my soul and my skills (if there were any useful) to the London Olympics. I must say I was surprised to be chosen as a drummer for the opening ceremony since I never ever played anything apart from the doorbell and occasionally my bicycle's horn. I am pretty sure with this curriculum I would have never been chosen to be a drummer at the Beijing Olympics, where almost identical drummers gave a perfectly executed rhythmic performance that not even the most idealistic Swiss watchmaker could imagine. Compared to them we looked like a bunch of messed-up folks: a bold English retired man, a two-metre-tall blue-haired Czech punk guy, a tiny Chinese woman, an athletic Afro girl, a Russian blondie and every single one of us had a complete different look, let alone individuality.

And this is the spirit I am talking about, what makes England so much English and yet so much open to diversity.

Everybody had equal chance to participate at the Olympic Ceremonies and thousands of people joined happily and we all represented the country together: from the Queen (despite the original suggestion that she could be played by a lookalike) to artists and professional performers (for a symbolical sum of £1), and thousands of English and alien volunteers. Amongst my favourites were the deaf children choir who sang the British national anthem in pyjamas, the copper petal carrier boy in a wheelchair, and those placard-bearer girls who weren't supermodels but average girls proud of their different look, different height, weight and size, even of their spots.

And that is England's spirit. It is seen when there is something larger than them going on. When they are welcoming the world and showing off their Englishness (or indeed Britishness), then they are at their most accepting. Not only tolerating differences but encouraging them.

And that is what I like about The English, because after all it is the combination of our differences and common humanity that makes the world a richer place.

29

HOW TO BE ARROGANT

'WRITING A BOOK is easy' people say. You just have to start writing the first sentence and then you write and write and write … until you finish the last sentence. And that's it.

I absolutely share this opinion. Well, to be honest I always undergo several nervous breakdowns and panic attacks between the first and the last sentence, but yes, apart from that it's pretty much the same process.

Writing a book is easy. Everyone can do it. But to publish it?! Well, that is what I call proper hard work.

George Mikes was lucky because his publisher, André Deutsch, was one of his best friends, they'd known each other since childhood when they both lived in Budapest.

Unfortunately I didn't play in the same sandpit with people who later became famous names in publishing, so when I thought it was time to approach the English book market with my first book (*One Way Ticket to London*) I had to do a lot of research to understand how the publishing business works in England.

Step One: I had to find a literary agent.

I realised quite soon that literary agents are a peculiar species. They are the hub of the universe. They are like God, who decide who goes to heaven and who can simply go to hell.

Literary agents are very eager to let you know on their websites that they are crazy busy and how much they hate writers who waste their precious time. Thanks to that I got extremely scared to send out submissions, because I didn't want to waste the agent's time by reading it, and waste more of their time by finding me a suitable publisher, then waste the publisher's time by publishing it and then the reader's time by reading it. In my nightmares I always pictured the worst scenario if my book become a worldwide bestseller I could see how depressed I would become to know that I wasted millions and millions and millions of readers' time.

Agents also have very strict rules about how they want to get your submission and if you don't send it according to their requirements they will just delete it without hesitation. Some of them accept submissions only by post, others only by email. Some want you to introduce yourself, others absolutely don't care who you are as they are just interested in your writing. Some want to read the first three chapters, some the first and the last chapter. Some want Ariel font with 11 font size, others prefer Cambria 12. If you send them your submission on Monday it will automatically land in the bin, since all agents hate Mondays. Some of them like getting and reading submissions on Tuesday at 9.42 a.m. with their breakfast, some of them on Thursday afternoon with their five o'clock tea, and the rest prefer reading novels on toilet so if they don't like it they can immediately recycle it and save the planet.

There are funny agent websites: 'we know that you and your family and all your neighbours and their dogs believe that your novel is a bestseller, but let us decide since we are the experts here.'

Some of them also advise you that in your professional writer CV (how can you have a professional writer CV if you are a first-time writer?) you should not mention that you were a publicist of some local magazine or you won any prize with your writing. They are only interested if you were the *Evening Standard*'s chief editor and you won a Man Booker Prize, apart from that you are just making yourself look ridiculous. Of course I didn't want to make myself look ridiculous, so my writer CV doesn't say such embarrassing things; just the pure truth that I am a qualified accountant with lots of experience in accountancy and finance, and I like writing in my lunchtimes.

Sometimes I also found agents that were helpful and keen to explain to writers how the publishing business works (because all writers are stupid, they don't know anything else apart from writing. According to agents they don't even know how to write either). This following explanation gave me lots of hope and self-confidence: Publishing business is like a fruit market. The agent is the shopper and I (the writer) am a banana. There are plenty of bananas and other fruits on the market. There is a small chance that the shopper wants a banana and even if they want it, that I will be the chosen one (especially nowadays when home delivery is increasing rapidly, isn't it?).

Since I was aware of this, every time I looked at the mirror I only saw a dark brown, rotten, loser banana. Even worst: loser alien banana.

Unfortunately the banana theory never works the other way round, like I (the writer) am the shopper and the agent is only one banana of the many other bananas (agents). Agents want to be treated special; they want to be The One. They want writers to send their submission only to them, and if they reject it, only then writers are allowed to send their submission to other agents. Some agent even intimidate writers, saying that publishing business is a small world and they talk to each other quite often so if they found out that I sent my submission to all agents in the same time they all will delete it, because I am wasting the whole publishing business's precious time. My first rejection arrived after a month and the last one after eight months. You don't need to be an accountant and good with numbers to realise that the strategy imposed by agents (send and wait for their answer, send and wait for their answer, send and wait for their answer ... etc., where 'answer' means: rejection) would have taken me nearly 50 years before reaching the bottom of my agents list. To be frank, I am not sure I am planning to live that long. As far as I know unsuccessful writers die quite young, most of them by suicide.

Instead of jumping from Tower Bridge I took a big breath, I followed all the other 'submission rules' and I approached 131 agents I felt suitable for my book in two weeks.

Being Hungarian (i.e. a born pessimist) I was ready for everything.

Most of the answers were nice, saying that my novel is not that bad and if I made some changes it could be a bestseller. By 'changes' they meant to put the words in a different order. I guess in such a different way that the new word order would actually result a completely new novel.

One day an agent rejected me (nicely) but asked me out for a date (even more nicely) and another replied 'it is not possible to provide UNSUCCESSFUL writers with detailed feedback' and then she wished me good luck and she hoped that I will succeed somewhere else and she hoped that she will hear about my success one day (Yes, I am sure, because that wouldn't mean that she failed as a literary agent, right?).

On that night I was so upset that I decided to self-publish my book. Why not, I said, this is the land of the DIY after all. Let the readers decide whether my book is a timewaster or not.

And you know what? In less than 100 days and with no marketing at all I manage to sell more than 3,000 copies. (Probably nothing for an agent but a lot for a little leftover alien banana.)

In the meantime a publisher (the kind of woman I would have loved to play in the sandpit in my childhood) contacted me saying that she had read my submission and unfortunately she doesn't publish such fiction books as *One Way Ticket to London*, but if I wrote something else she would be interested since she thinks I have a sense of humour similar than that George Mikes had.

I couldn't believe what I just heard!

A couple of years ago I had had exactly the same idea: to write an update of George Mikes' *How to be an Alien* on what happened to The English since 1946, but all the people (aliens) I talked to about my plan said it was an extremely arrogant idea.

So I asked the English publisher the same question: 'Don't you think it is arrogant to think I am capable of updating a worldwide bestseller?'

All she said was: 'Yes.'

And this is how I learnt that being arrogant is an offence among aliens, but a compliment among The English. English people are proud of their arrogance. Being arrogant is a must if you want to succeed, and not just in the publishing business but everywhere in England.

And this is the story how I became arrogant, and the story of how this book was published.

Will I write more books?

Of course I will.

I absolutely share George Mikes' thought about writing:

'I do not quite know why this should give us satisfaction but it does. Writing keeps us from more criminal activities. A new book is our just revenge on the world.'

P.S. In case you find any contradictions in my book.

A. *If you are an alien:*

Blame The English. They are the contradictory. It was impossible to write a book about them without contradictions.

B. *If you are English:*

You shall blame yourself.
I know it is a pleasure for you.
You are welcome.

AFTERWORD

WHILE I WAS finishing this book I was on sabbatical leave in Hungary. It was the peak time of the refugee crisis for those fleeing Syria. There were lots of moments when I deeply felt ashamed of being a Hungarian. I even promised myself that I would never move back to my homeland, which seemed like a country of inhumanity and hate.

But at the same time, even though it wasn't in the international news, I realised Hungary was full with humanity and love. There were wonderful Hungarian people who welcomed refugees at train stations and volunteered to help.

I was at Budapest Keleti Train Station on my way back from a family visit when I first saw those Syrian aliens, people who weren't leaving their country just like I did, free to jump on an airplane and move to another country, but were escaping from death through a painful journey, sometimes treated as they were the problem and not the consequence of the true problem: the war. It was shocking and deeply moving. Of course I knew about the Syrian civil war and the millions of refugees, but reading words and numbers about their situation and looking into a three-year-old refugee girl's eye sitting on the cold pavement is two different thing.

At that moment all I could do was break out into tears and to hand over all Mum's home-made cookies and to run away. I was traumatised and extremely frustrated for not being able to save all those refugees.

But then I accepted the fact that it is true: I cannot help all those people. But at least I can help certain people at a certain moment, just as everyone else could. And that would make the difference.

So I packed blankets, clothes and my childhood dolls into bags and headed back to the station, where I was happy to see other Hungarians arriving with donations.

On the way home from the station I decided that the following day I would buy 50 pretzels for the Syrian kids camping at the station.

I was naive. Living in England for a decade somehow made me expecting the refugee children forming a happy queue and calmly wait for their turn to take one pretzel each. It didn't happen that way ...

And this was the moment when I realised how much I love queues.

And this was the moment when I understood the philosophy of queuing. That standing peacefully in a queue means *peace* itself. You can only stand patiently in a queue if you know that there are enough pretzels for you and for everyone, if you have enough money to buy as many pretzels as you wish, and if you have enough time to wait for your turn. If any of those conditions is missing, you cannot stand peacefully in a queue.

I truly wish that by the time you are reading this words all the refugees will stand peacefully in a queue waiting for their pretzels, not as a charity food in an alien country but in a bakery in their beloved homeland. Because if that happens, it will mean peace.

Angela Kiss is a writer and accountant. Born in Hungary, she has lived and worked in London for ten years. She has had three books published in Hungary, one of which was her memoir, *One Way Ticket to London*, which has been translated into English and self-published as an ebook.

If you have enjoyed this book and would like to find out more about Angela Kiss or our other authors, please visit www.septemberpublishing.org and follow us @septemberbooks.

September is an independent publisher; curating, collaborating and championing.